The New Americans
Recent Immigration and American Society

Edited by
Steven J. Gold and Rubén G. Rumbaut

A Series from LFB Scholarly

Beyond the Immigrant Enclave
Network Change and Assimilation

Susan Wierzbicki

LFB Scholarly Publishing LLC
New York 2004

Copyright © 2004 by LFB Scholarly Publishing LLC

Library of Congress Cataloging-in-Publication Data

Beyond the immigrant enclave : network change and assimilation /
Susan Wierzbicki.
   p. cm. -- (The new Americans)
 Includes bibliographical references (p.) and index.
 ISBN 1-59332-004-3 (alk. paper)
 1. Minorities--United States--Social conditions. 2. Immigrants--
United States--Social conditions. 3. Social networks--United States.
4. Acculturation--United States. 5. Assimilation (Sociology)
6. Community life--United States. 7. United States--Ethnic relations.
8. United States--Social conditions--1980- I. Title. II. Series: New
Americans (LFB Scholarly Publishing LLC)
 E184.A1W45 2004
   305.9'06912'0973--dc22

2004006934

ISBN 1-59332-004-3

Printed on acid-free 250-year-life paper.

Manufactured in the United States of America.

Table of Contents

List of Tables

Acknowledgments

All those who have helped me have my deepest gratitude.

I thank the Office of University Partnerships at the U.S. Department of Housing and Urban Development, which provided me with a grant. The Ford Foundation sponsored me at a seminar at the University of Michigan to learn about the Multi-City Study of Urban Inequality. The seminar, run by Irene Browne in June 1999, was invaluable in helping me get started. I thank Rubén G. Rumbaut for encouraging me to publish in this series and Leo F. Balk for his graciousness and patience.

Many people have read and commented on this work along the way. In particular, I would like to thank Avery M. "Pete" Guest and Charles Hirschman, whose extensive and excellent comments improved my work substantially and whose support has been invaluable. Others who have generously extended their suggestions include Paul Burstein, Mark Ellis, Kristin Espinosa, Becky Pettit, Kate Stovel, June Strickland, and Suzanne Davies Withers. Martina Morris, Jerry Herting and Justin Baer offered statistical advice. David M. Grant provided additional data. Carolynn Bramlett cheerfully helped with word-processing. Finally, I thank Frank D. Bean for his great counsel, concern, and generosity.

CHAPTER 1
Immigrant Networks

Et tous ensemble
Dans cet hôtel
Savons la langue
Comme à Babel

Fermons nos portes
A double tour
Chacun apporte
Son seul amour

(Guillaume Apollinaire, "Hôtels")

When Apollinaire wrote of boarding-house life, "We fasten and then bolt each door / Bearing self-love and no more," he understood the potential loneliness of the unattached sojourner. While isolation and alienation have long been staple literary themes, they also emerged as central themes in social research on early 20th-century immigrants. Despite the importance of ethnic churches and other immigrant institutions, social scientists long portrayed European immigrants as uprooted, unacculturated and alone (e.g. Thomas and Znaniecki 1984, Wirth 1938, Handlin 1952), struggling to make the transition from peasant *Gemeinschaft* to urban *Gesellschaft*.

Yet research over the last 40 years has countered many of these early social-science views by showing immigrant communities as tightly knit, often around these same ethnic institutions. The rise of network research has provided a supply-side argument for the importance of transnational social ties in determining patterns of migration (Massey et al. 1987, Massey et al. 1998) and a fruitful new focus for immigration studies in general. Labor research has illuminated employers' reliance upon their own or their workers' ethnic networks in filling job openings (e.g. Portes and Bach 1985, Bean and Bell-Rose 1999) and creating ethnic niches. By pointing out that immigrants are self-selected for social ties (else they would not have migrated), some scholars have concluded that immigrants probably have closer, stronger social ties than natives and that interdependence among immigrants preserves these ties (Waldinger 1999).

In the past few years, however, sociologists have begun to examine the circumstances under which ethnic communities become dense and solidary – or do not. This new line of research represents a return to old sociological questions, in that it recognizes that structural factors neglected in or tangential to the study of transnational migration networks may in fact be crucial to understanding immigrant adaptation. For example, research into chain migration does not distinguish sending from receiving networks, though such networks can vary with the reasons for immigration and expectations of long-term settlement (Tilly 1990). Rather, the theory describing the development of transnational networks suffers from what Waldinger describes as "inevitabilism" (1999: 229): Networks that can provide jobs to untold numbers of compatriots seem to sprout from the migration of one low-status person, without any explanation of how these outsiders enter and then ascend the social structure. Moreover, in linking networks to the concept of social capital, network theory does not allow for the possibility that social capital can even be negative if new arrivals place heavy demands on the older ones. Nor does it account for the context of reception, which influences social relations among immigrants (Menjívar 2000, Portes and Rumbaut 1996, Portes and Sensenbrenner 1998), or variation by class, race and especially gender of immigrants (Pessar 1999). Last, transnational-network theory generally omits discussion of ecological context, in part because of the difficulty of determining the proper spatial framework. If enclaves are an inadequate lens for examining the entire immigrant experience (Portes and Bach 1985, Waldinger 1993, Y. Zhou 1998), the rise of the U.S. service economy and movement of manufacturing suggests that the metropolitan area and even nation may be too myopic a scale as well (Sassen 1990, Smith 2001).

Recognition of these shortcomings in migration-network theory has laid the groundwork for development of a more synthetic account of immigrant adaptation, involving class, race, gender, politics of reception, social capital and ecological context. The concept of segmented assimilation, providing for different mobility paths for immigrants' children, exemplifies this new approach, because it frames the social mobility of the second generation in terms of race, social capital and place. Segmented assimilation also represents a return to the study of social networks at the local level, the locus of the Chicago School's landmark studies of immigrant adaptation (e.g. Wirth 1956). Segmented assimilation further recognizes the interaction of neighborhood and network, particularly in impoverished areas. This recognition suggests potential for comparison of the social and spatial mobility of poor immigrant minorities with poor native minorities.

Within the United States, the structural and ecological framework for poverty, expounded by Wilson in *The Truly Disadvantaged* (1987), generally is applied only to native African-Americans rather than immigrants. Wilson stresses the isolation of the poor in ghettos and their limited information and access to jobs as a result of economic restructuring. Here, too, a debate has emerged on whether Wilson's framework should apply to immigrants. Some scholars have argued that an underclass does not develop in *barrios*, in part because Hispanic immigrants have extensive kinship ties and in part because most *barrios* have not experienced the severe poverty described by Wilson in Chicago ghettos (Moore and Pinderhughes 1993). Others have argued that enduring educational inequality among Mexicans (Hirschman and Falcon 1985) and other Hispanic groups stems from segregation and discrimination and from the resulting (though not inevitable) development of oppositional attitudes. In such circumstances, Wilson's conception of permanent poverty as both structural and spatially bounded is appropriate for minority immigrant groups (Zhou 1999), although oppositional attitudes may have more to do with class than immigration status (Perlmann and Waldinger 1999).

So to understand immigrants' experiences at their destination, a synthetic account might examine immigrants' networks (or, more broadly, their social capital), the ascribed characteristics that place them in a structural framework, their achieved characteristics (which may also be considered human capital), and the spatial context. These kinds of studies are rare. Because of the relative ease of examining the spatial distribution of people rather than their networks, most large-scale, quantitative research on immigrants has tended to *substitute* spatial location for networks as a way of measuring of interethnic contact, and this crude proxy is a source of potential bias. Indeed, ethnographic studies have shown that ethnic minorities in the suburbs often are left out of local social life (Gans 1967, Fischer 1984: 263), not integrated into it. Thus the relationship of networks at the destination to spatial location remains a relatively unexplored area.

Beyond these questions on immigrant adaptation lies another: how the act of immigration itself and the context of reception might affect social networks. If immigrants leave most family members behind, they may have to rely more than natives on friends or neighbors for network contacts, or they may forgo many relationships in the expectation of returning home soon. If many immigrants from a particular country lack green cards or face a hostile reception, they would probably have fewer institutional resources and would be more likely to fall prey to exploitation from fellow immigrants. Further, the preference of people for others like themselves would predispose immigrants to seek out fellow immigrants, but the availability of similar people varies by context (Huckfeldt 1983). The extent to which immigrants then choose dissimilar people for strong ties might provide insights into information bridges (Bienenstock et al. 2000) and potential routes for assimilation.

Sociological research has yet to provide a broad, quantitative approach to examining immigrant networks among a variety of ethnic groups and neighborhood types. Yet the growing proportion of immigrants in the United States would make such a study ever more salient and useful for understanding social and labor patterns among people who have had to position themselves within the social structure of a new country. This volume begins to fill that gap by comparing immigrants to natives in the number of strong social ties, the types of relationships represented by those ties and the level of homophily in the ties.

Immigrants' ability to forge primary relations with other members of other racial and ethnic groups forms the linchpin of traditional assimilation theory. Milton M. Gordon (1964:70) called the development of these primary relations "structural assimilation" and defined it as entering "fully into the societal network of groups and institutions" of others. Newer forms of assimilation or incorporation theory (e.g. Alba and Nee, 2003; Bean, Stevens and Wierzbicki, 2003; Brubaker 2001) have refined Gordon's canonical account. Still, the idea of structural assimilation, or the crucial ability to enter broader social networks, remains vital to an understanding of immigrants' economic mobility (Portes 1995). Yet despite the fundamental importance of network ties for assessments of incorporation theory, relatively few researchers (e.g. Laumann 1973; Tilly 1990; Portes 1995) have analyzed assimilation in network terms.

The role of neighborhood in immigrants' ties is especially intriguing in light of recent research showing that many first-generation immigrants are sufficiently well-to-do to settle upon arrival in integrated, middle-class neighborhoods (Tseng 1995; Zelinsky and Lee 1998; Logan, Alba, and Zhang 2002). In the traditional assimilation model, spatial assimilation stems from acculturation to the language and values of the host society and from socioeconomic mobility (Massey 1985). Because wealthy immigrants have scarcely have had time to acculturate, spatial assimilation may not serve as an intermediate step in their structural assimilation. For this reason, spatial assimilation does not always suffice as a *proxy* for structural assimilation. Using spatial assimilation to measure structural assimilation assumes that physical distance is tantamount to social distance, though the nature and extent of the relationship remains a long-running theoretical and empirical question. Studies of suburbs have shown that ethnic minorities who have spatially assimilated often remain socially isolated in their new neighborhoods and rely instead on longstanding but now spatially distant ties (Gans 1967; Fischer 1984). Network perspectives stress that social ties extend far beyond any given neighborhood or, in the case of immigrants, beyond even national boundaries (Massey et al. 1987, 1998; Wellman and Wortley 1990; Waldinger 1993; Zhou 1998; Zelinsky and Lee 1998).

New assimilation theory

The concepts of assimilation and incorporation have recently undergone re-examination and reformulation after a generation of criticism (Alba and Nee, 2003, 1997; Bean et al., 2003; Brubaker 2001; Kazal 1995). Although classic assimilation theory never involved unadulterated predictions of Anglo-conformity, its implication that "straight-line" change would occur among immigrants has been put to rest by the findings of segmented-assimilation research (Zhou and Bankston 1998; Portes and Rumbaut 2001), which show how ethnic networks can structure the incorporation of the children of immigrants into different economic strata. New works (Alba and Nee, 2003; Bean et al., 2003) recast assimilation in less sequential terms, as the result of individual decisions and collective action in densely tied groups. Crucial change comes through the blurring of boundaries between groups, and this depends on the groups' close and continuous contact, reinforced by institutions that uphold civil rights. Brubaker (2001) notes that the unit of analysis consists of multiple generations, not the individual, and that these populations need to be thought of as heterogeneous across many dimensions instead of homogeneous units. Assimilation then involves a change in the distribution of the immigrant generations of a group across these dimensions so that their distribution comes to resemble the distribution of dimensions within a reference group.

Such new structural conceptions of assimilation extend Gordon's (1964) framework. Gordon distinguishes seven dimensions of assimilation in a way that lent the previously imprecise concept of assimilation to empirical analysis. The first dimension is acculturation, or change in cultural patterns. The second, which Gordon (1964: 81) calls the "keystone to the arch of assimilation," is structural assimilation, or widespread primary relations between groups and full entrance into the social networks and institutions of others. Structural assimilation will automatically spur the other dimensions of assimilation: intermarriage, unity of identification, absence of prejudice, absence of discrimination, and absence of power conflicts.

Empirical analysis of assimilation has long focused on Gordon's types of assimilation, since several dimensions of assimilation (e.g. intermarriage) readily lend themselves to being operationalized. However, the "keystone" of structural assimilation itself has been either neglected as a measurement or operationalized in terms of socioeconomic status. Because structural assimilation is related but not conceptually identical to the other kinds of assimilation, the use of other kinds of assimilation as indicators of structural assimilation leaves open the question of construct validity. For instance, evidence already suggests that identificational assimilation does not parallel other kinds of assimilation and socioeconomic incorporation (Neckerman, Carter, and Lee 1999; Bean et al., 2003). A direct indicator of structural assimilation is necessary not only to uphold Gordon's conceptualization but also to allow empirical testing of segmented assimilation and the micro-level interactions that collectively shape the institutionalist perspective on assimilation. Such an indicator could be membership in ethnic or non-ethnic networks, which have been used considerably in examining ethnic employment (e.g. Bailey and Waldinger 1991) but less so in terms of general social contacts. Ethnographic work on immigrants (e.g. Zhou and Bankston 1998) has amply shown the importance of networks in socioeconomic mobility among immigrants.

In particular, the work of Peter M. Blau (1977) may contribute to an understanding of Gordon's idea of structural assimilation. Although Blau is not directly concerned with assimilation, he argues that group size and internal variation among groups matter for intergroup contacts. The importance of different structural dimensions also matters. If groups become more heterogeneous along salient dimensions, they should have more cross-cutting contacts and more evidence of the exact sort of structural assimilation that Gordon was talking about. A truly assimilated society would have randomly distributed contacts – and that does not happen – but the assimilation of any ethnic group might be considered under way if its level of intergroup contact approximates that of a reference population, contingent upon the size of the group.

Homophily

Homogeneity in strong ties is more formally known as homophily, or the "birds-of-a-feather" attraction of people similar in attitudes and backgrounds. Contained within the principle of homophily are related assumptions: that people associate with members of different groups even though they nonetheless associate disproportionately with members of their own group. Of course, the groups themselves vary in homogeneity, with the variation depending in large part upon the relative size of the group and the density of contacts among its members (Blau 1977; Rytina and Morgan 1982; Blum 1985). Homophily may cover many dimensions, depending on people's self-concept and socialization to any particular reference group (Laumann 1973; Lin 2001). This paper focuses mainly on one dimension, that of race or ethnicity, because of the importance and scope of the debate over the intersection of race/ethnicity and immigration status (McPherson, Smith-Lovin, and Cook, 2001; Bean and Bell-Rose 1999; Rumbaut 1999).

Why examine homophily? Homophily can represent social mobility or indicate the level of integration among different groups. The more that groups are alike along nominal parameters, the more likely are in-group relations; the weaker the correlations among the parameters, the greater the likelihood of intergroup relations (Blau 1977: 144). Because strong parameters along a number of dimensions – linguistic, cultural, often racial – distinguish immigrants from natives, immigrants would be expected to show high levels of homophily; they are the classic Simmelian "strangers." Attenuation of such strong parameters would indicate social incorporation.

However, the idea of homophily as an indicator of immigrant incorporation remains mostly unexamined. More often, social integration is measured at the individual level socioeconomically through income or education (Neidert and Farley 1985), spatially through residential settlement patterns (Massey and Denton 1987; Alba et al. 1997, 1999), culturally through language retention (Stevens 1992, Espenshade and Fu 1997) or structurally through intermarriage rates (Gordon 1964; Kalmijn 1998; Fu 2001; Rosenfeld 2001). The level of homophilous strong ties would not necessarily measure the acceptance of an immigrant group by a native majority (such acceptance being a necessary part of structural assimilation), but it would capture the level of the immigrants' intergroup ties. Portes (1995: 25) argues that "the limits and possibilities offered by the polity and the society at large can be interpreted as the *structural embeddedness* of the process of immigrant settlement; the assistance and constraints offered by the co-ethnic community, mediated through social networks, can be defined as instances of *relational embeddedness.*"

The concept of homophily captures the micro-level intersection of structural and relational embeddedness. Homophily can both support or constrain immigrants. Great similarity and overlap in strong, primary relations such as kinship or friendship may provide social and emotional support (Litwak and Szelenyi 1969; Wellman and Wortley 1990). At the same time, homophily closes off "bridges" to new information from diverse social networks (Fernández Kelly 1995). Such bridging usually comes from weak, instrumental ties, unless the individual lacks a variety of acquaintances, in which case any bridging has to result from strong ties (Granovetter 1973, 1982). A *strong* tie that is also heterogeneous probably indicates that the respondent is linked to diverse social networks in ways that go much further than mere intergroup contact. Social ties do not develop in a vacuum but from already existing social ties or around specific foci (Feld 1981), so that new contacts tend to be similar to existing contacts. In this way, homophily or heterogeneity in social networks tends to perpetuate itself.

Neighborhood in particular can influence the composition of social networks (Blackwell and Hart 1982; Huckfeldt 1983; Fernández Kelly 1995). Homogeneous environments can constrain intergroup relations even when the participants have few in-group preferences (Blum 1985), since all potential friends are basically alike. However, studies vary widely on the effects of neighborhood heterogeneity on social relations within the neighborhood (for reviews, see Greenbaum and Greenbaum 1985; Lee and Campbell 1999), and most neighborhood studies focus on black-white relations and omit consideration of immigrant groups. By contrast, the literature on immigrant neighborhoods generally assumes homogeneity in social ties. Early studies portrayed second-generation working-class enclaves as dense and solidary (e.g. Gans 1962; Suttles 1968), with multiplex social relationships. More recent works have shown that communities with closed networks can provide social support and social capital (Portes and Bach 1985; Zhou and Bankston 1998). Ethnic enclaves tend to be portrayed as buffer zones that re-create familiar institutions and allow use of the mother tongue. If such enclaves are institutionally complete, immigrants need not interact much with the native population (Breton 1964; Gordon 1964).

Dense ethnic ties are not a given among immigrants, as several studies have shown (Bodnar 1985; Mahler 1995; Menjívar 2000; Ochoa 2000; Portes and Rumbaut 2001).

The salience of different ascriptive or achieved parameters can determine the level of group solidarity (Blau 1977). For instance, declining discrimination against Asian-Americans has reduced the importance of the parameter of race and led to greater class-based division (Espiritu and Ong 1994). Pessar (1999) argues that unequal gender relations preclude true ethnic solidarity. An ethnography of Koreans in Los Angeles concludes that "solidarity remains more rhetoric than reality" because of class schisms, a lack of leadership, personal and political feuds within voluntary associations, denominationally divided churches, and little local coverage of Korean-American news (Abelmann and Lie 1995: 107). In particular, Yancey, Ericksen and Juliani (1976) identify four conditions that reinforce kinship and friendship networks and ethnic solidarity: common jobs, residential stability and concentration, and dependence on shared institutions and services. Because all these structural parameters introduce variability into the types of social networks forged by immigrants at their destination, the structure of social networks offers insight into the process of social incorporation.

Strong ties within social networks

Membership in social networks and other social structures provides the mechanism by which individuals can attain their goals. The social ties that comprise these networks range from weak acquaintanceships to strong emotional commitments, and each type serves a different function. Weak ties to other social networks (which can be quite numerous) may offer information, social control and some social bonds. But the poor, who often lack weak ties, must rely on their relatively fewer stronger ties for job leads and other social bonds (Granovetter 1973, 1982). These strong ties generally refer more to the kin, friends and neighbors, who provide both instrumental and expressive support. They handle large and small services, long-term commitments, aid in emergencies, companionship and overall emotional support (Litwak and Szelenyi 1969, Wellman and Wortley 1990). Such support provides strong psychological benefits and protects against the effects of stress (see Ahlbrandt 1984). Strong primary ties tend to predict political involvement (Burstein 1976; Guest and Oropesa 1986), but they may not always advance the individual's economic interests (Stack 1974).

Besides benefiting the individual, strong ties serve a macro-level function as well. As Gordon (1964) argued, the development of primary relations with other groups is the keystone of classical assimilation theory. While Gordon expected that most immigrant groups would experience this type of assimilation, he saw it by no means as inevitable. Rather, he noted that many ethnic groups could provide lifetime networks and associations that would minimize any necessity of primary relations outside the group. Note that the argument about assimilation or ethnic retention assumes the existence of primary ties; the question is with whom the immigrant forms the ties.

The massive evidence for chain migration and cumulative causation of immigration (Massey et al., 1998) has tended to sweep aside sociological arguments that would militate against heavy involvement of immigrants in social networks. If immigrants used networks to decide where to migrate, to find housing and land a job, how could they possibly fail to have strong social ties?

Yet except among immediate family, where strong ties may be present from birth, actors have to develop strong ties from among their acquaintances. Making friends depends on the chances of similar individuals to interact, because interaction generally leads to positive feelings, while lack of interaction breaks them down (Homans 1950). The biggest predictors of adult friendship are similarity of status and demographic traits and spatial proximity (Verbrugge 1977). These traits hold true for both same-race and interracial friendships (Hallinan and Williams 1989). Of course, proximity does not necessarily mean sharing a neighborhood or workplace. Adults can intermingle in a variety of social settings: commuting, shopping, pursuing recreation and so forth, and that variety appears to be growing. In fact, since the mid-70s, survey evidence shows a slight increase in socializing outside of neighborhoods and less within neighborhoods (Guest and Wierzbicki 1999). But for several reasons, immigrants may face singular barriers to interaction among themselves and with others.

First, social distance and shifting identities among immigrants themselves may hinder the formation of strong ties. Simmel (1950) saw the migrant as a stranger whose relation to a group was predetermined because he had not initially belonged to that group and because he introduced to the group qualities that were not inherently there. Immigrants arriving at their destination have to renegotiate their identities and roles.

On a broader level, first-generation immigrants pursuing friendships with co-ethnics may encounter class divisions within the immigrant cohorts (Yancey et al. 1976, Abelmann and Lie 1995). While multiculturalists stress the vitality of ethnic-group institutions, those immigrants whose identity is not strongly tied to the ethnic group may not partake in those institutions. If so, they might have few strong social ties. Indeed, failure to recognize agency would be to conflate immigrants as a group with immigrants as a category. A group engages in activities and sets membership criteria; its members would have dense networks. But a category or ethnic designation exists because others associate individuals with that category regardless of the individuals' involvement in group activities.

Second, language may be a barrier to widespread social ties. Immigrants may not only be unable to speak English, they may have only a rudimentary grasp of the language or languages of their native country. Some immigrants are ill-educated; others speak dialects. Their children may speak a patois of English and their native tongue and choose not to communicate in the immigrant language. All these factors would limit the pool with whom the immigrant can develop strong ties.

Third, the work setting for many immigrants may provide little opportunity for strong ties. An immigrant in a manual job may have little invested in the job itself and little in common with co-workers as a result. In fact, the same workers may be competing for jobs, especially if older, more established cohorts feel edged out by younger ones. Moreover, some common occupations among immigrants, such as domestics, are highly isolated (Hagan 1998). Finally, some poor laborers working long hours lack the leisure or the energy for socializing (Mahler 1995, Furstenberg and Hughes 1997).

All these reasons suggest that social ties among immigrants may vary considerably in their strength and density. Despite the popular image of the immigrant enclave as a nurturing hive, poor immigrants in reality may be isolated spatially and socially in ways analogous to the poverty perspective invoked by Wilson in ghettos. To begin to address that question, this volume compares immigrants' and natives' strong ties.

The volume will further the discussion on the nature of

networks among immigrants in several ways. First, it examines the level of strong social ties, or primary expressive relations, among some groups of Hispanics (primarily Mexicans) and some Asians, the majority of whom are first-generation immigrants and groups less studied in network analysis. It puts these ties in an urban spatial context. Second, it shows the level to which immigrants rely on kin and friends for strong ties and whether immigrants differ from the native-born in the similarity of their ties. Such differences would illuminate structural limitations on the ability of immigrants to form bridges with dissimilar people. Third, the volume links immigrants' social networks to structural and place-based frameworks for explaining poverty. It does this by examining the spatial distribution of social ties within a community network perspective (Wellman 1979, Wellman and Leighton 1979).

The community network perspective consists of a heuristic framework for examining the spatial distribution of social ties as neighborhood-based or more far-flung. It is simple and perhaps even simplistic, and Wellman himself has refined it considerably (e.g. Wellman and Potter 1999). But this perspective remains useful because it explicitly questions the extent to which social relations are confined to the neighborhood. Because research about the effect of ties centered on the neighborhood has become ever more popular and because results have diverged widely, the community network perspective is important to avoid *a priori* assumptions about where ties are located.

The volume is organized as follows. Chapter 2 links social networks to urban context. It also looks at the meaning and importance of social ties, particularly to immigrants. Chapter 3 shows the prevalence of strong ties among different ethnic groups, neighborhoods and cities. It further looks at the trade-off between neighborhood context and individual characteristics in determining the presence of strong ties. Chapter 4 examines whether immigrants or the native-born have more ties with kin. Chapter 5 looks at ties by residence among co-ethnics for both immigrants and the native-born. Chapter 6 explores the similarity of ties along several dimensions, including race/ethnicity, education level and marital status, to see for which groups dissimilar ties might be most likely. It further examines the importance of neighborhood in fostering such ties. Chapter 7 expands on the community typology for immigrants and connects social networks to assimilation

Data are drawn from the Los Angeles segment of the Multi-City Study of Urban Inequality (MCSUI), a stratified survey that oversampled poor and minority populations in Detroit, Atlanta, Boston and Los Angeles (Bobo et al. 1998). In Boston and Los Angeles, the oversampling of poor and minorities is tantamount to an oversampling of immigrants, which makes the MCSUI one of the few sources of data on a variety of immigrant groups. The sample size and breadth in Los Angeles are particularly useful. As a primary port of entry, Los Angeles attracts a variety of Asian immigrants, while its proximity to Mexico has given it the largest Mexican population in the country.

One important finding in this volume is that regardless of racial or ethnic group, immigrants report significantly fewer strong social ties outside their own households than do the native-born. On the one hand, one might expect such a finding – after all, even if social ties are a necessary precondition for migration, why should immigrants, especially those with little money or education, have as many social ties as the native-born? On the other hand, the finding contradicts the "common knowledge" that immigrants are especially good at looking out for one another. Indeed, a furniture manufacturer whose workforce had become largely Hispanic through employee referrals said, "I don't want to sound racist, but I never met a lonely Mexican. They all have extended families" (Waldinger 1999: 243). Of course, an outsider would never have occasion to meet a Mexican who lacked family or friends to make the introduction. Thus, that employer's assumption that no Mexicans are lonely was based on acquaintanceship with Mexicans who were self-selected for their strong ties. Such perceptions are commonplace and make this volume necessary.

CHAPTER 2
Community as Networks and Place

Since the beginning of sociology as a discipline, researchers have struggled to understand the relationship between social ties and neighborhood (see review of recent works in Lee and Campbell 1999). In the mid-20th century, research tended to characterize neighborhoods by the types of ties of their residents, so that, for instance, slums were equated with alienation and ethnic enclaves with bounded solidarity (Shaw and McKay 1942, Gans 1962). Less discussed was the conflation of neighborhood with resident; not every slum dweller was atomized nor every enclave resident thick with neighbors and kin. In the 1970s, social network analysis shifted scholarly attention to sets of social ties, and research began to view social ties as more structural than bounded by space. Moreover, spurred by a new emphasis on weak ties (Granovetter 1973), other work began to focus on how strength of ties related to their function. These new trends overwhelmed discussion of neighborhood, so that only within the last 15 years has work begun to link networks to neighborhood effects. Even in this age of easy international communications, network research shows that most contacts remain, as they always have been, among people who are physically close to one another (Wellman 1996). Especially in poor neighborhoods, which may lack access to outside resources, close-in ties may still be quite salient.

This chapter overviews the connection between community defined as networks and community defined as space. The first section discusses the meaning and importance of social networks at the macro level and social ties at the micro level. It focuses specifically on the provision of strong ties and their role in providing social support and the effects of their absence. The next section expands upon the typology of community delineated by Barry Wellman (1979) and the macro/micro linkages of networks and neighborhood context. The last section relates immigration to the community typologies and presents a theoretical approach.

The meaning of social ties

While controversies abound over the definition of "community" (see Brint [2001] for a recent overview), three major thrusts seem to have emerged. One is to define community as a place, as in the community studies tradition. The second is the elective community of people who share common interests but do not necessarily know one another, such as the "environmental community" or "Republicans." A third type is the personal community consisting of the network of friends and acquaintances of any individual. Even though these concepts are distinct, they are not mutually exclusive, since people tend to seek out others like themselves. This volume begins with the third definition of community – as sets of personal networks – and examines how the spatial conception of community interacts with it.

The structural approach of network analysis focuses on "concrete social relations among specific social actors"

(Wellman and Berkowitz 1988: 5). Network theorists organize individuals by their location within a structure (Wasserman and Faust 1994, White, Boorman and Brieger 1976). They explain collective action in patterns of linkages among interest groups and coalitions and ultimate access to resources. By contrast, other macro-sociological theories of social structure depend more on categories or membership within groups. For instance, Blau (1977) argues that intergroup relations depend largely on group size, with smaller groups interacting with outsiders more than larger groups. For Blau, the correlation among parameters, ascriptive or achieved, determines the rates of in-group cohesion. These two approaches are more complementary than contradictory. Group parameters tend to explain more how social structure is created and provide a framework for the intersection of social and spatial ties. Networks explain more how social structures are linked.

In network analysis, networks bind people into a coherent structure of durable relationships that connect social units and explain constraints on human action. Individuals are not autonomous but connected, and these connections permit the transfer of resources. Individual connections, or social ties, may be weak and specialized, in that two people interact only for one purpose, or strong and multifaceted, involving many different types of social support. Similarly, the *sets* of ties that comprise an entire personal network vary in number and strength across individuals.

Because no two networks are identical in size and shape, networks provide different levels of resources. Individuals' ability to use their membership in networks as a resource is the essence of social capital (Coleman 1988, Portes 1998). That is, people with more connections and more skill at using them enjoy more advantages. Networks are therefore necessary but not sufficient for the creation of social capital.

How this social capital actually relates on the micro-level to the strength of individual social ties remains a matter of disagreement (Burt 2001, Portes 2000, Sandefur and Laumann 1998). One argument looks at social capital mainly as information. In this view, weak, "bridging" ties between groups are vital to passing along information and to keeping networks vital (Powell and Smith-Doerr 1994, Granovetter 1973). A second, nearly diametrically opposed argument casts social capital in terms of trust. In this view, dense ties and networks in which members generally know one another build trust and solidarity and provide social control (Coleman 1988, Portes and Sensenbrenner 1998, Granovetter 1985, Zhou and Bankston 1998).

Ronald S. Burt (2001) tries to reconcile these viewpoints of social capital as built through both weak, open networks and strong, closed ones. He argues that much of the evidence for the value of closed networks has stemmed largely from studies of children, for whom constraint is valuable (see Zhou 1999). By contrast, adults benefit more from weak ties that bridge networks, because such ties provide information about business opportunities. Of course, these ties cannot be too weak, or no one would have enough trust to exchange information.

Even so, adults need strong ties, too, because these ties provide social support. The notion of social support has proven hard to define, but the consensus appears to be that "social support refers to interpersonal transactions which are designed to help the individual" (Antonucci and Knipscheer 1990: 164). (For a summary, see Lin 1986.) Nan Lin distinguishes two kinds of social support: instrumental and expressive. Instrumental actions are those in which the goals are separate from the means (e.g. job-seeking), whereas expressive actions are those in which the goals are tantamount to the means (e.g. sharing life experiences).

According to Lin, these instrumental actions can take place at any of three layers of structural relations: a broad "community" that provides a sense of belonging, personal networks providing actual linkages, or an inner layer of confiding partners with whom reciprocal exchanges take place. With instrumental action, wider networks offer more potential resources from which to draw, so the individual is more likely to attain goals. Granovetter's famous insight on the "strength of weak ties" (Granovetter 1973) shows that job-seeking information often comes from weak ties that represent bridges to other social networks.[1] But instrumental action is only part of social support. Only through the expressive side of social support does a network help individuals cope with personal difficulties and stress. In fact, a large sociological literature supports the hypothesis that social resources buffer life stress (Lin and Ensel 1989).

Expressive action generally takes place at the inner layer of confiding partners, or strong ties. A social network is a necessary but not sufficient means to attaining social support. Rather, Pearlin et al. (1981: 340) argue that "the final step depends on the quality of the relations one is able to find within the network. The qualities that seem to be especially critical involve the exchange of intimate communications and the presence of solidarity and trust."

The question remains whether these strong ties must be homophilous. Based in part on George Homans' theory that

---

[1] Granovetter (1973: 1361) defines the strength of a tie as "a (probably linear) combination of the amount of time, the emotional intensity, the intimacy (mutual confiding), and the reciprocal services which characterize the tie."

interaction, sentiment and activities are self-reinforcing, Lin operationalizes social support as "access to and use of strong and homophilous ties" (Lin 1986: 28, Homans 1950: 120). But some research suggests that homophily should not be incorporated into the concept of social support. For instance, a heterogeneous social network has been found to have a positive effect on preventive health behavior (Hüttner, Franssen, and Persoon 1990). For this reason, an operationalization using *only* the presence of a strong, confiding relationship (e.g. Thoits 1984) seems less likely to assume that homophily is automatically part of a strong tie. Rather, the level of homophily is more likely to be an empirical question, especially since homophily can cut across several dimensions.

Another unanswered question is the status of people with few or no social ties. From the rise of *Gesellschaft* to Durkheimian suicides to Simmel's stranger to uprooted Polish peasants, social isolation has been a leitmotif in sociology. Faris (1934) introduced a health angle by showing that isolation from intimates, particularly in "disorganized" communities, is linked to schizophrenia. Yet for all that traditional absorption with social integration, relatively few studies have examined the social correlates of isolates (Fischer and Phillips 1982).

The work by Fischer and Phillips finds that social networks are complex and that the correlates of isolation interact. Isolation from non-kin is common among those of low socioeconomic status: the poor, the unemployed, the unschooled. Isolation from kin is commonplace among those who have recently moved. Marriage promotes kin relations for both women and men, but especially men. Marriage isolates women from non-kin, while age tends to isolate men. Ultimately, isolation seems to be a function of lack of access to different types of social contexts.

As Wilson (1987) has argued, another correlate of isolation is neighborhood. He finds that ghettos are more isolated than they used to be because of greater inequality between ghettos and other neighborhoods. When middle-class blacks had no choice but to live in a ghetto, social inequality was greater within ghettos, but the middle class maintained social and economic ties to more mainstream institutions. The flight of the black middle class isolated the poor. In Blau's terms (1977), as the status differences between the ghetto and other neighborhoods grew, so did the barriers to social relationships. Spatial segregation then reinforced these barriers. Although Wilson's macro-level theory does not address social isolation *within* the ghetto, the characteristics of many ghetto residents (poor, unemployed, ill-educated) correspond to the characteristics of social isolates found by Fischer and Phillips (1982). Moreover, net of individual traits, residents of disadvantaged neighborhoods tend to be more mistrustful (Ross, Mirowsky and Pribesh 2001). It is therefore possible that ghetto residents are isolated not only from members of mainstream institutions but also to a large extent from one another. If so, social isolation at the macro level has atomized ghetto residents.

But whereas Wilson's argument for blacks in the ghetto stresses social isolation, much of the prevailing theory for immigrants in the enclave stresses an abundance of social ties. Studies of immigration networks tend to focus on social capital obtained through closed networks building trust and solidarity (e.g. Portes and Bach 1985, Zhou and Bankston 1998). Where ethnic enclaves offer a range of institutions, immigrants may preserve their mother tongue and avoid interactions with the native population (Breton 1964, Gordon 1964). Such accounts of ethnic solidarity can verge on the oversocialized. For instance, Pieke (in Massey et al. 1998: 182) says that Chinese immigrants seldom integrate with non-Chinese or even Chinese from other areas; instead, "new immigrants enter a ready-made social environment: employment, friends, relatives, recreational patterns, way of life, and career pattern are to a large extent predetermined."

The popularity of the studies explaining transnational chain migration may reinforce the presumption of a multitude of ties among immigrants. A theory of chain migration developed in part to counter the inadequacies of neoclassical economics in explaining migrant flows. The theory depends upon self-reinforcing transnational networks (Massey et al. 1998). As these networks grow, migrants gradually build personal, social and economic ties to the receiving society and yet maintain relationships in their homeland (Massey et al. 1987). These dual ties allow for the exchange of information and money and encourage further migration. This theory is intended to explain how social ties affect who migrates at origin, so it really does not apply to social ties at destination. Nevertheless, the success of theory hinges upon one of two assumptions: that the networks that encouraged migration remain intact and supportive at the destination or that the broader community institutions (the outer layer of community in Lin's [1986] terms) will muster sufficient instrumental aid to sustain newcomers. If time and poverty have attenuated social ties or if the community lacks institutions, social networks cannot be self-reinforcing.

In fact, the level and cohesion of networks within immigrant communities appears to vary. Social capital among immigrant communities may depend upon the level of exterior discrimination and interior resources (Portes and Sensenbrenner 1998). Confrontation with the host society can produce tightly knit ethnic communities, such as the

Chinatowns that developed in the wake of the Chinese Exclusion Act and both residential and employment discrimination (Zhou 1992). However, discrimination can also produce overlapping affiliations in response, as in the case of Korean entrepreneurs facing discrimination as middleman minorities. They forged pan-ethnic and class-based alliances in addition to forming Korean business organizations (Light and Bonacich 1988). At the same time, the salience of different ascriptive or achieved parameters within the group can determine the level of group solidarity. Class and gender divisions may undercut ethnic solidarity. Institutions may prove more fragmented than cohesive

In the Children of Immigrants Longitudinal Studies, Portes and Rumbaut (2001) find that Nicaraguan and Mexican families in particular often report that co-ethnics have given them virtually no support. They blame different socioeconomic backgrounds and types of reception in the United States for the variation among immigrant communities. As an example of an "atomized" immigrant household, they cite this case (with fictionalized name):

"The interviewer asked Señora Santos if she thought people from Mexico help each other here. The question elicited an emotional response in her. Tears came to her eyes as she expressed her disappointment that Mexicans as a group are not tight-knit like the other immigrants who work together and help each other. She cited jealousy and selfishness among people of her own group which alienated them from each other. 'If they can't have it, they don't want anyone else to have it either. Not like the Vietnamese who cling together,' Señora Santos said. 'Listening to her,' noted the interviewer, 'I had the impression that this was a very lonely woman.'" (Portes and Rumbaut 2001: 111)

Thus, from the macro level of group solidarity through the more meso level of social networks within and across groups, the social structure among immigrants is more of an empirical question than a given. Immigrants may lack well-grounded social networks. On the other hand, immigrants are unlikely to be as socially isolated as the black population described by Wilson. Hardly any immigrant groups have been as segregated as Midwestern blacks or faced as much discrimination in the mainstream economy (Lieberson 1980). Yet the ill effects of low socioeconomic status may still isolate some immigrants, particularly if they belong to a group that faces hostility from the native-born. The question becomes one of degree of isolation in comparison to the native-born.

Advancing the network-analytic perspective

For immigrants at the place of destination, a useful way of framing types of potential ties stems from the network-based work of Wellman (1979), who characterized communities as "lost," "saved" or "liberated." The community "lost" is the oldest. It dates from Tönnies (1963 [1887]), who argued that urbanization and industrialization had altered the nature of attachments from communally based *Gemeinschaft* to associationally organized *Gesellschaft*. In turn, Louis Wirth (1938) argued that the size, density and heterogeneity of the city loosened the bonds of local community and attenuated kinship-based primary ties. The community "lost" is often associated with social disorganization. In the community "lost," local ties do not cease but are weak and narrowly defined. Though such ties might provide acquaintanceships, they would provide little actual support.

Since the 1960s, more research has supported the other type of local community, the "saved" (Kasarda and Janowitz 1974, Fischer 1984). In this view, solidified, localized communities persist because they help residents negotiate formal bureaucratic structures and provide social control and job skills (Wilson and Portes 1980, Zhou 1999). Such communities would be critical to immigrants in need of human capital, or the skills to get a job on their own within the receiving city. The community "saved" offers overlapping social circles of kin and childhood friends with many strong local ties but few external ties (Gans 1962, Suttles 1968). Many immigrants see their place of origin as community "saved" and may tend to romanticize their memory of it (Menjívar 2000; see also Lomnitz 1977).

The rise of network analysis in the 1970s led to the delineation of the third type of community, "liberated." In this conception of community, ties are ramified and mostly independent of neighborhood. Liberated networks boast multiple strong, primary ties, as well as weak ties, in differentiated networks. By conceptualizing community as a network instead of a place, the community "liberated" represents a rejection of the ecological approach.

Although such widely dispersed ties have been found in U.S. immigrant communities as early as the mid-19th century (Scherzer 1992), only fairly recently have scholars applied the liberated networks to immigrant groups. For example, Zelinsky and Lee (1998) identify as "heterolocalism" the existence of an ethnic community in the absence of an enclave, and they *define* the term in part through its liberated social networks. Thus, their heterolocal immigrant community exists *only* through ramified networks, since it is independent of spatial bounds. In this heterolocal community, immigrants promptly disperse upon arrival. They work, live and often shop in separate districts, yet maintain ethnic ties by telephone, visits, community groups, churches, and other means. This is possible in part because new immigrants in general are more skilled than before and often know at least some English (Smith and Edmonston 1997). They immigrate with human capital and sometimes financial capital, too, and need not rely exclusively upon co-ethnics. Ultimately, socioeconomic status, not ethnicity, determines residency (Zang and Hassan 1996, Hwang and Murdock 1998).

Of course, Wellman's communities represent an ideal type; there is room for middle ground. Communities of co-ethnics can vary in their network orientation across the same city (Oliver 1988). Many neighborhoods show elements of the community "saved" and "liberated." Guest (2000) argues for the importance of both localized and non-localized ties in understanding that social organization is multidimensional. This becomes important to remember so as not to set up a "straw man." Thinking of the community "saved" or "liberated" as *the* type of community among immigrants can perpetuate a myth that the enclave sheltered all immigrants and that everyone within an enclave belonged to the same ethnic group. Spatially, only blacks and Chinese have ever been highly segregated (Lieberson 1980). More often, the enclave housed a minority of the immigrant group, and often those immigrants were only a plurality, not a majority, in the enclave itself (Philpott 1978). Thus, immigrant communities exist across a spectrum of spatial concentration from highly segregated to highly dispersed. Any recent trends toward "heterolocalism" represent a change in degree across these two dimensions, not a wholesale change in immigrant relations.

Just as middle ground exists between the three typologies of communities, so, too, does middle ground exist between the definition of community as place and as network. In the 1970s, network theorists broke with human ecology, but in the 1990s, burgeoning numbers of studies on neighborhood effects restored a long-standing sociological connection between networks and neighborhoods. This neighborhood-effects literature is inconclusive, however (see Furstenburg and Hughes 1997). In an attempt to bridge micro- and macro-level conceptions of community, Freudenburg (1986) and Sampson (1988) view density of networks and social cohesion as community-level properties in and of themselves. Tienda (1991) has suggested defining neighborhoods first in social terms and secondarily in spatial terms as a way of proceeding conceptually and ultimately empirically with such research.

Likewise, it is possible to recast Wellman's community typology both socially *and* spatially. With community "lost," the social aspect is weak and transitory, so the community is often defined spatially. This is definitional shorthand, however. The "lost" part refers to social ties, not spatial boundaries. Even though an unusual proportion of social ties within a neighborhood may be unstable, it is not the neighborhood that is "lost" but the personal networks of some proportion of residents. In fact, Fernandez and Harris (1992) find evidence of social isolation in the ghetto, but only at the personal level and *not* at the neighborhood level. More generally, Wilson's (1987) study of the spatial isolation of the ghetto underclass represents a now classic example of community "lost" because many residents may lack outside contacts and possibly even strong ties within the ghetto. Klinenberg (2002) argues that more people, especially men, risk isolation as a larger proportion of the population ages alone, but he also blames isolation on the loss of public spaces and supported housing in poor areas and a culture of fear. Other community-lost studies also show how mistrust permeates particularly poor neighborhoods and keeps social relationships distant and private (Rainwater 1970, Merry 1981, Kasinitz and Rosenberg 1996).

In the case of community "saved," the social and spatial boundaries of community are roughly the same. In such enclaves, residents have little privacy because of the multiplexity of social ties: Friends are neighbors and co-workers. Although many seminal studies of the community "saved" focus on the social relationships within working-class neighborhoods (Bott 1955, Gans 1962, Keller 1968, Suttles 1968), this type of community also applies to some ethnic enclaves. Zhou and Bankston (1998) cite the social control over Vietnamese youth in Versailles Village in Louisiana, because all the parents know one another.

In community "liberated," the relationship between spatial and social boundaries is more complicated. The community liberated is often portrayed as aspatial and thus at odds with the traditional Chicago School axiom of spatial distance equating to social distance. But this is a false dichotomy. In the community liberated, the spatial dimension shapes the social dimension, but only loosely. Face-to-face interaction – on which strong ties with non-kin often hinge – depends on the propinquity of the actors (Mouw and Entwistle 2001, Wellman 1996, Sigelman et al. 1996), regardless of whether the setting is a neighborhood, office or some other institution. While strong ties in the liberated network also can exist independent of space, such ties require more effort to maintain. Moreover, propinquity does not work alone but in tandem with the social environment. For instance, someone living where a particular social class is dominant would be more likely to have friends from that class, regardless of the subject's own status (Huckfeldt 1983). Neighborhoods with a high mean proportion of friendship ties foster more neighborhood ties (Sampson 1988).

Despite the spatial effects in all three types of communities, it would be illogical to apply Wellman's typology to a place, because only individuals can have social ties. Yet within any given neighborhood, the social ties of a preponderance of residents may be of one type. Just what kind of ties flourish where is a debated empirical question. For instance, dense, neighborhood-based social ties traditionally have been associated with the working class (Bott 1955, Laumann 1973, Suttles 1968, Gans 1962), but some more recent work suggests that most ties are liberated regardless of the class of the neighborhood (Bridge 1995).

One landmark study that examined both place and social networks involved interviews with more than 1,000 adults in 50 communities in northern California (Fischer 1982). The clearest network findings were that education and income strongly influenced both the size and composition of networks. The higher the respondent's education and income, the greater the number of ties overall and the greater the reliance on non-kin ties. "These findings challenge the romantic notion of working-class or lower-class sociality. The poor people we interviewed not only lacked friends, they also tended to be involved with fewer relatives than were the middle-income respondents" (Fischer 1984: 252). Although Fischer was drawing from only a small sample of blacks and Chicanos, he found that they tended to have smaller, less supportive networks. The clearest ecological findings were that urbanites tended to rely more on non-kin than kin and to have less dense networks, i.e. with fewer of their associates knowing one another. Urbanites also had less traditional beliefs and attitudes, though many of the differences could be traced to self-selection.

Immigration and the community typology

The history of Wellman's community typology might as well be a history of immigration. The immigration literature parallels – if not actually inspires – the theoretical basis for the communities "lost," "saved," and "liberated." Thomas and Znaniecki's study of Polish peasants (1984 [1918-20]) describes immigrants as both demoralized and yet communal, so that those who did not belong to a variety of groups or institutions might be isolated indeed. In such a work lie the seeds of both community "lost" and "saved." The concept of community "lost" rose to prominence first through studies of disorganization in ethnic neighborhoods. Drawing on other studies of the Chicago School, Louis Wirth argued in his often cited essay on "Urbanism as a Way of Life" (1938) that migrants to the city faced a bombardment of stimuli such that they had to retreat from interaction with others. Oscar Handlin (1952:4) said that "seen from the perspective of the individual received rather than of the receiving society, the history of immigration is a history of alienation and its consequences." But studies of immigrant communities actually refuted much of this typology. Wirth's own description of the ghetto (1928) seems more like a community "saved," with strong, local institutions, gradually becoming a community "liberated."

By the 1960s, studies of immigrant communities such

as those by Gans (1962) and Suttles (1968) of second-generation Italian neighborhoods, had established community "saved" as the dominant type for immigrants. It remains so, bolstered by studies like those of modern Chinatowns (Zhou 1992) or Vietnamese enclaves (Zhou and Bankston 1998). Still, the suburbanization of immigrants, especially in places like Los Angeles, has fostered some theorizing that immigrants are forging liberated networks from the start (Zelinsky and Lee 1998). Moreover, the rise of transnational networks of immigrants sustains an image of a broader community that is very liberated.

Yet, despite all the research attention to the role of networks in chain migration (e.g. Massey et al. 1987), several recent studies suggest that the type the community "lost" was perhaps jettisoned too quickly. Not all immigrants necessarily belong to well-connected networks. Since network research by design locates people within networks, it would be easy for network researchers to conclude that all people are in networks, even if some are only marginally connected. If immigrants have to re-create social ties at the destination, as Tilly (1990) suggests, some may be unable to do so. Creation of social ties may be particularly difficult if the immigrants as a group had faced a reception that was indifferent or even hostile. In that case, competition among immigrants may outweigh cooperation and exacerbate class schisms.

Several studies of immigrants (Bodnar 1985, Mahler 1995, Roschelle 1997, Menjívar 2000) show how economic competition supersedes ethnic and even familial bonds. Mahler describes how established Salvadoran immigrants on Long Island exploit desperate newcomers, who become embittered and suspicious:

"Migrants undergo two forces simultaneously: centripetal obligations toward relations in the host country and centrifugal obligations toward those in the home country. Since migrants share the compulsion to produce surplus income, they understand that they are unlikely to be completely severed from their friends in the United States if they send home remittances. ... But the price they pay is that there will not always be someone to help them in times of need. Thus, shortly after arriving in the United States, many people were disappointed by their relatives' behavior. The kind of hospitality and common courtesy they expected was suspended here; they saw people less as a community to rely on than as individuals to compete against for success in the immigrant game." (Mahler 1995: 101-102).

Of course, Mahler's sample may not be generalizable. The Salvadorans were peasants dislocated by war, received with hostility, and, mostly, alone. Expecting to return home soon, many Salvadorans migrated without their families. They were unused to a market economy, had no skills besides farming, and found that the only path to social mobility consisted of exploiting fellow migrants. Because they worked as much as possible, they had little spare time for socializing or supporting voluntary organizations. As a result, Mahler concludes that the immigrants she studied "seem to stand closer to the anomie side of the solidarity-anomie continuum" (Mahler 1995: 222). She criticizes the prevailing models of ethnic solidarity as overly romantic. Last, she warns that in their efforts to counter the anti-immigrant literature of the first part of the 20th century, researchers must beware of overcorrection.

Menjívar and Roschelle document how poverty undermines reciprocal kinship exchanges, which are especially important among women. In her ethnographic work on Salvadorans in San Francisco, Menjívar (2000) argues that immigrant networks become destabilized – and thus the production of social capital stops – in the face of adverse immigration laws, a poor economy and a lack of community resources. She lists several often overlooked features of immigrant networks. Among them:

- Social ties used in migration may weaken at the point of destination. As a result, migration networks may need to be distinguished from settlement networks.
- Ties to the same people are not uniformly weak or strong but vary by time and context.
- In the absence of resources, network ties will not automatically create social capital.
- Internal group divisions inhibit the development of ethnic solidarity.
- The context of reception changes the dynamics of networks.
- Social networks need to be viewed as endogenous rather than exogenous.

Roschelle's (1997) <u>No More Kin</u> refutes the classic ethnography <u>All Our Kin</u> (Stack 1974), which argued that poverty motivated poor black women to form dense exchange networks of both nearby kin and non-kin as a survival strategy. Roschelle says that extreme poverty undermines the ability to offer reciprocal exchange and thus the very networks themselves. She argues that contrary to the notion that extended networks of kin and friends nurture minorities, it is non-Hispanic whites who report having the greatest extended social support networks. She finds that Puerto Ricans, a highly disadvantaged group, are the least likely to give help despite a culture that values duty toward family.

These works suggest that socioeconomic status in part structures the nature of immigrant ties. They suggest that newly arriving immigrants can count on friends and relatives only a little when the former might be just scraping by, and that acquaintances, in fact, may exploit the newcomers' labor because newly arrived immigrants have no other sources of job information. This idea of exploitation harks back to studies of mistrust and isolation in the black ghetto (Liebow 1967, Rainwater 1970, Wilson 1987). Exploitation is an adaptation to structural constraints; it is not part of a culture of poverty. But exploitation is very much in keeping with the perspective of the long-dismissed community "lost."

These works constitute a critique of part of the prevailing network theory of migration. That theory expresses the importance of the shared experience of migration as reinforcing social ties (Massey et al. 1987: 140). Close kin, longtime friends, and *paisanaje*, or the sense of belonging to the same community of origin, all help cement networks. These ever-developing networks provide jobs, housing, food and social life at the destination. In more naïve descriptions, the development of immigrant networks proceeds arithmetically. At the same time, host-country discrimination restricts networks to fellow migrants and fosters ethnic solidarity. In more nuanced accounts, the context of reception varies.

These two approaches – that of poverty and networks – can co-exist within the same immigrant groups. Some immigrants may enjoy dense networks of kin and friends. Some may feel isolated and mistrustful. What proportion of any particular group that appears to be isolated or well-connected is an empirical question that has not really been addressed among first-generation immigrants. Yet it is an important question, because it speaks to a potential hidden lack among immigrants of information and social support. It is the question addressed here.

Using survey data, this volume examines the number, type, and similarity of strong ties outside the household among immigrants as compared with the native-born. Strong ties indicate the broader social circles in which immigrants move, so the extent of strong ties is a reasonable proxy for the existence of supportive networks. (For further discussion of this point, see Appendix B.) Within this framework, I test the effect of socioeconomic factors along with race and other demographic covariates as a way of determining how much poverty is related to the number of strong ties. I use the word "poverty" in its broadest sense, to refer to a lack of resources; these include income as well as education and employment.

If the results show that a large proportion of the immigrant population reports no strong ties outside the household, this would indicate the presence of a community "lost." If the results show that a lack of ties is associated with low socioeconomic status, this would indicate that the same structural mechanisms associated with the old community "lost" may still be in place for immigrants. The literature on ghettos links poverty to isolation (Wilson 1987) and residential mobility to lack of neighborhood cohesion (Sampson 1988). Large numbers of immigrants are poor and unskilled in English, and being migrants, they are often mobile. It would follow that patterns of isolation similar to those in black ghettos might crop up among such immigrants. Certainly, the ethnographies of Menjívar and Mahler strongly suggest this for Salvadorans.

The typology of community "lost" is easy to criticize. Wirth (1938) sets up isolation as a consequence of urbanization, even though subcultural theory (Fischer 1984) holds that urbanites are more likely than rural residents to find others who share their interests. But criticism of community "lost" along urban/rural lines does not negate the existence of isolation. A second criticism equates isolation has long been equated with social disorganization, a term that easily gets linked to a culture of poverty. But isolation is structural and therefore distinct. It is also easy to see isolation as complete, even though relatively few people lead truly hermetic lives. But if people are not close to anyone else, they are isolated, no matter how many others with whom they exchange pleasantries or information. They are like Eleanor Rigby, of whom Paul McCartney sang, "died in the church and was buried along with name/Nobody came" (The Beatles 1966). Finally, immigrant communities are often portrayed as particularly close, with many extended kin nearby, so that despite their poverty, they do not conform to Wilson's model of isolation (e.g. Moore and Vigil 1993). But if community "lost" refers to a personal community and not a place per se, that criticism is beside the point. Within any neighborhood may live people with few, if any, strong ties. So in spite of criticism, the idea of community "lost" has persisted, especially in the literature on deviance and race relations. Moreover, the concept of community "lost" also may apply to immigrants, especially if that concept is updated to frame community from a networks perspective as well as an ecological one.

In such a framework, characteristics of the neighborhood can contribute to the location and type of strong ties, i.e. kin or non-kin. But the neighborhood itself is endogenous, since demographic characteristics such as race or the presence of children as well as income all contribute to the choice of neighborhood. While it is possible to measure neighborhood characteristics as an aggregate of the demographic characteristics of the residents, it is much more difficult to measure the sense of attachment to community or the institutional opportunities for participation. Yet for those people who are not place-bound, the community atmosphere is crucial to determining the level of commitment and the proportion of social ties that stay within the neighborhood (Albrandt 1984). The true effect of neighborhood is therefore difficult to gauge but important to try to measure.

For immigrants in particular, neighborhood may be important, especially if the immigrants are poor or unable to speak English. They would be heavily place-bound and at a great disadvantage if their neighborhoods did not offer opportunities for interaction. One such institution is the soccer club, which has proven enormously popular as a gathering place for Mexican immigrants (Massey et al. 1987). Yet immigrants are often still transient and unsettled. Residential mobility is the greatest drawback to social cohesion (Sampson 1988). Especially among newer and poorer immigrants, the presence of such institutions cannot be assumed.

My general hypothesis is that adversity (defined as a general lack of resources that constrain opportunity) keeps many immigrants from being able to form strong ties outside the household. I will test this using data on race/ethnicity, immigration status, demographic characteristics, education, income and neighborhood characteristics. The null hypothesis, of course, is that poverty has no relationship to the presence of strong ties.

This null hypothesis more or less corresponds to immigrant-network theory, which also expects no effect from poverty, since it emphasizes how immigrants can rely on friends and kin to help them get by. In this way, I am contrasting a poverty perspective with immigrant-network theory. Chapter 3 explicitly tests these models.

Building on Fischer's findings (1984), I further expect that adversity will inhibit the development of ties with non-kin. This could be especially problematic for immigrants, since they may have left close relatives behind at the place of origin and thus have fewer kin to fall back on. Again, this contrasts with immigrant-network theory, which assumes that either friends or relatives will be around. Adversity should also influence whether ties are with neighbors or not, since poor people may have less ability to get around. Chapters 4 and 5 test this set of hypotheses.

I also expect immigrants to be more racially and ethnically homophilous than the native-born. This is because immigrants are so distinctive along many salient parameters (Blau 1977) and have so many shared experiences. However, here the effect of neighborhood should be stronger. Immigrants' neighbors are not always fellow immigrants. But the more ethnically similar the neighborhood, the more likely the immigrant to associate with someone of the same ethnic or racial background. These effects are tested in Chapter 6.

CHAPTER 3
The Presence of Strong Ties

The literature on social ties within immigrant communities contains two distinct camps. One camp holds that immigrant communities consist of dense, solidary networks of co-ethnics, in part because most migrants are self-selected at the origin for their far-flung networks. Immigrants draw upon these networks for help with employment, information and social support. This approach is illustrated by studies of enclave solidarity (Moore and Pinderhughes 1993, Massey et al. 1987, Zhou and Bankston 1998), job leads (e.g. Bailey and Waldinger 1991; Waldinger 1999; Sanders, Nee, and Sernau 2002) and transnational linkages (Schiller 1999, Portes, Guarnizo and Landolt 1999). The second camp stresses the debilitating effects of poverty and economic competition among immigrants and suggests that socioeconomic status should influence the number of social ties among immigrants (Menjívar 2000, Mahler 1995, Roschelle 1997). This camp not only examines the *nature* of immigrants' social ties, it questions the very *existence* of such ties. Little research has directly compared these two approaches (but see Portes and Rumbaut 2001), even though their assumptions are fundamental to the framing of the immigrant experience. This chapter draws attention to that

Beyond the Immigrant Enclave

gap and begins to address it, by examining both the quantity and quality of strong ties outside the household among the native-born and foreign-born among three racial and ethnic groups in Los Angeles County.

The network theory of migration suggests that migration networks remain strong and intact at the destination. At a macro level, this model assumes ethnic solidarity. Migrants rely on these networks of kin or friends in deciding whether and where to move and later in receiving help with housing and jobs. Waldinger (1999) explicitly mentions how the very act of migration can sustain these networks by providing a shared experience. The critics of this viewpoint stress the difficulty of sustaining old social ties or forging new ones in the face of an adverse reception, poverty and economic competition within the immigrant group. Their focus, however, has been on immigrant groups like the Salvadorans, whose migration from a war-torn country was traumatic, whose applications for legal status were often denied, and whose avenues for help were limited until co-ethnic institutions began to grow in the late 1970s and 1980s (Hamilton and Chinchilla 2001). But the finding of diminished networks even among less beleaguered groups, such as the Puerto Ricans (Roschelle 1997), suggests that this adversity perspective may apply more broadly to other groups besides Salvadorans. These differences between the network and adversity perspectives lead to testable hypotheses:

1 Network perspective: Because immigrants are self-selected for their social ties, most should have strong ties at their destination.

Adversity perspective: Where the first generation of a group is poorer and less educated than its native-born co-ethnic counterparts, the first generation should have fewer overall strong ties. Controlling for socioeconomic status should attenuate these differences.

2   Networks: The longer the time at the destination, the more immigrants should become embedded in a co-ethnic community and develop strong ties.

Adversity: Socioeconomic status, rather than length of residence, determines the ability of immigrants to forge strong ties.

These hypotheses are not mutually exclusive but depend on different mechanisms.

The Los Angeles context

The study focuses on Los Angeles County, whose status as a premiere port of entry and whose large and longstanding Mexican population make it the best place in the country to compare the foreign-born and native-born of an immigrant group. Los Angeles County has no ethnic majority (see Table 3.1). It is the nation's largest magnet for Mexicans and Central Americans. Its Asian population outnumbers its black population. The Asian immigrants hail mainly from China, the Philippines, Korea, Vietnam and India, in that order (Waldinger and Bozorgmehr 1996). Segregation levels between blacks and whites in Los Angeles County remain high, though they have fallen since 1970, while segregation levels between whites and Hispanics have generally grown (Clark 1996). Asian groups tend to have settled in widely separated clusters, with the result that they tend to be even more segregated from one another than from non-Hispanic whites (Cheng and Yang 1996).

Table 3.1   Population of Los Angeles County, 1990, by nativity and race/ethnicity

	Proportion of adult population[a]	Proportion of population that is foreign-born	N	Total population all ages[b]
Total		.405	4,025	8,863,164
Non-Hispanic White	.448	.158	861	3,634,722
Non-Hispanic Black	.126	.103	1,118	946,862
Hispanic[c]	.364	.733	994	3,306116
Mexican or Mexican-American	.268	.672	697	2,519,514
Salvadoran	.034	.972	125	253,086
Asian[c]	.061	.880	1,052	928,710
Chinese	.025	.952	532	248,415
Korean	.023	.992	353	143,674
Japanese	.012	.522	163	132,261

a. First three columns based on the Multi-City Study of Urban Inequality (MCSUI). However, the MCSUI does not disaggregate Asians by ethnicity, whereas the original Los Angeles study did. My thanks to David M. Grant for providing data on individual ethnic groups.

b. From Summary File 3 of the 1990 Census of Population, all ages.

c. Individual groups within these categories are tallied if their observations total more than 100. The survey did not sample Filipinos, so data for them are unavailable.

L.A. County's vast and growing Mexican-origin population (2.5 million in 1990), once concentrated in East Los Angeles and Azusa, has merged almost into one residential area. Mexicans have moved into the once heavily black areas of South Central Los Angeles, Watts, Compton and Inglewood. Other concentrations in the San Fernando Valley are growing (Ortiz 1996).

Most of the Salvadorans and Guatemalans are refugees, many of them unauthorized. As a smaller population, they have not formed enclaves of the same magnitude as those from Mexico. Although the area of Pico-Union/Westlake is known for its Central American population, fewer than 10 percent of the Salvadorans and Guatemalans in the Los Angeles area live there. Instead, 60 percent of the Salvadorans live in census tracts that are predominantly Latino but are less than 10 percent Salvadoran (Lopez et al. 1996).

Among Asian groups, there are several distinct areas of settlement. One is the old central district, around Little Tokyo, Koreatown, Chinatown and the area near Monterey Park, which is now known for its Chinese population, although Japanese had settled there earlier. Another settlement area is the county's southeast corner (a more mixed area with Chinese, Koreans and Filipinos). Because early Japanese farmers had settled in Gardena, in the South Bay area, the suburbanization of this area attracted more Japanese-Americans as well as Koreans. Koreans and Filipinos also have settled in the San Fernando Valley (Cheng and Yang 1996, Allen and Turner 1997).

As Table 3.1 shows, the great majority of many specific ethnic groups are first-generation immigrant. However, there is one important exception: those who identify themselves as Mexican-Americans. Among them, fewer than 10 percent are foreign-born. By contrast, those identifying themselves as simply Mexican are 98 percent foreign-born. The Japanese are another group with a substantial native-born proportion. Salvadorans, Chinese and Koreans are well over 90 percent foreign-born.

The Multi-City Study of Urban Inequality (MCSUI)

Data for this study come primarily from the Multi-City Study of Urban Inequality, a major in-home survey of adult urban residents in four cities: Detroit, Atlanta, Los Angeles and Boston from 1992-1994 (Bobo et al. 1998). To minimize cultural bias in face-to-face interviews, investigators relied on co-ethnic interviewers wherever possible. This study focuses on the Los Angeles segment of the study, because it was the largest at 4,025 respondents and contains the most immigrants. I draw on some of the Boston results by way of comparison, because they provide face validity to the totals. Because the study focused on inequality, it oversampled census tracts with concentrations of poor and minorities.

A caveat is in order. No data set is perfect, and the limitations of the MCSUI preclude a full-scale test of many of the theoretical ideas set forth in the previous chapters. Yet this appears to be the best public data available now on immigrants, their networks and their neighborhoods. Other data sets follow immigrant networks, but they are designed to follow linkages among immigrants and cities rather than focus on neighborhood context. I chose the MCSUI because it is a multi-stage, clustered probability survey, geolinked to 1990 census data. By providing random samples by type of neighborhood, this survey picks up social isolates and avoids the selectivity bias inherent in data-gathering approaches that collect network information only on those persons with certain kinds of ties (Marsden and Hurlbert 1987). No other data set appears to permit such detailed network and neighborhood information, at least for adults (data on adolescents' networks are quite rich). The advantages are that one can glimpse some of the differences in network structures between first- and second-generation immigrants in adulthood and sample immigrant populations that could not be picked up in school-based surveys because they did not attend high school. The tradeoff is more limited information than in some other surveys on the social ties ("alters") named by respondents. For more information on the survey instrument, see Appendix A.

The crucial variable consists of a question meant to elicit the respondent's core social network by asking for discussion partners. The actual MCSUI question reads:

> "From time to time, most people discuss important matters with other people. Looking back over the last six months – who are the people, other than people living in your household, with whom you discussed matters important to you? Please tell me the first name or initials of the people with whom you discussed matters important to you. IF LESS THAN 3, PROBE: Anyone else?"

This is a variation on the important-discussant question first used in a special module of the General Social Survey (GSS) in 1985. While the wording of the "important-discussant" question can be criticized as vague and hard to interpret, the very ambiguity of the question was what attracted researchers to it in the first place, because it "identifies comparatively intense portions of the interpersonal environment for all respondents, and it thus has some general utility" (Marsden 1987: 123). Moreover,

at least three recent studies tend to confirm its validity
(Blau, Ruan, and Ardelt, 1991, Bailey and Marsden 1999,
Straits 2000). For more informationon, see Appendix B.

Table 3.2   Percentage distribution of ties with discussion partners in
             Los Angeles and Boston, by race/ethnicity and nativity

Number of ties	None	One	Two	Three	Total	N
Los Angeles						
Mexican	38.3	8.0	12.1	41.7	100.0	697
Native-born	29.1	12.6	14.4	43.9	100.0	180
Foreign-born	42.8	5.7	10.9	40.6	100.0	517
Chinese	53.8	4.9	11.0	30.3	100.0	532
Native-born	30.7	5.7	5.8	57.8	100.0	30
Foreign-born	54.9	4.8	11.3	29.0	100.0	502
N-H Black	23.4	10.2	18.8	47.6	100.0	1,118
Native-born	25.2	11.1	15.8	47.9	100.0	1,073
Foreign-born	7.4	2.6	45.1	45.0	100.0	45
N-H White	11.1	6.1	17.5	65.3	100.0	861
Native-born	10.4	6.0	18.9	64.6	100.0	735
Foreign-born	14.5	6.6	10.3	68.7	100.0	126
Boston						
Puerto Rican	32.6	33.1	15.5	18.8	100.0	351
Dominican	55.8	11.7	9.5	19.3	100[a]	217
N-H Black	20.1	7.4	22.3	50.1	100[a]	409
N-H White	8.3	7.7	20.3	62.6	100[a]	487

[a] This total may not exactly equal 100 because of missing cases.

Because the naming of confidants is a question that
often requires probing by interviewers, it is particularly
prone to interviewer effects (Marsden 2003). For this
reason, I compare marginal results in Los Angeles to those
in Boston, because the two cities had different interviewers,
different training of interviewers and different placement of
the network module in the survey questionnaire. See Table
3.2.

Results for non-Hispanic blacks and whites are remarkably consistent across the two cities. In Los Angeles, 11.1 percent of non-Hispanic white respondents reported no confidants, 8.3 percent did in Boston. In Los Angeles, 65.3 percent of whites reported three or more confidants., while in Boston, 62.6 reported three or more. In both cities, blacks reported fewer ties overall than whites, and the differences were consistent. Latinos reported even fewer ties, and here the variation was wider; however, different national-origin groups were involved. Among Mexicans in Los Angeles, 38.3 percent reported no confidants outside the household, while in Boston, 32.6 percent of Puerto Ricans had no ties, and 55.8 percent of Dominicans. The general consistency across cities gives these results some face validity.

However, it is not possible to compare Asians across the two cities, and the Asian sample in Los Angeles appears to show unacceptable levels of interviewer effects. Of the five people who interviewed the most Asians (accounting for nearly 39 percent of the total interviews of Asians), four reported no network data for overwhelming proportions of respondents. Nor was this pattern confined to only these five interviewers. For example, one interviewer provided network data for only one of his 64 Asian respondents. This interviewer and some of the others also interviewed non-Asians, though not so many, with similar gross omissions of network data. The extent of these interviewer effects among Asians compromises the quality of the network for this racial group and introduces noise into the overall sample. Because of the difficulties with the data, I present marginal data for Asians but generally confine statistical analysis to other groups.

Following previous work (Marsden 1987, Straits 1991, Louch 2000), I am using the "important-discussant" question as a proxy for strong ties. This is not a perfect proxy. First, many people do not discuss "important matters" even with close friends. Many of their friendships may actually fall into what Wireman (1984) calls "intimate secondary relationships," in which people may be friendly within a given context (e.g. a soccer club or church) but never develop an external relationship. A study among white urban men finds that friendships tend "to be rather circumscribed affairs in which there are relatively restricted exchanges of intimate content" (Laumann 1973: 125). Because of these limitations, my measurement may be omitting some ties marked by deep loyalty but constrained conversation. Second, the exchange of confidences is only part of the definition of a strong tie (Granovetter 1973). These ties often have instrumental components as well, which are not necessarily captured by a question on important discussants. To help determine whether the discussion partners are indeed strong ties and whether strong ties might mean something different to immigrants or the native-born, I examined a further question from the MCSUI: "Is person [1,2,3] someone you could count on for help in a major crisis, such as serious illness or if you needed a place to stay?" Consistently, across groups and among the foreign-born and native-born, approximately 80 percent of respondents reported that they could count on the confidant they had named in a crisis.

Substantively, both race and nativity matter greatly in the distribution of strong ties, as Table 3.2 shows. Among whites, nearly two-thirds report having at least three strong ties outside the household, and nearly 90 percent have at least one such tie. The proportions for the black and Mexican-origin population are much lower. Among the Mexicans and Mexican-Americans, 38 percent report no strong ties outside their households. Among the Chinese, more than half – nearly 54 percent – report no strong ties, though this surprising finding must be discounted because of interviewer effects. Among three groups, the distribution is bimodal, showing generally no ties or three or more. As a result, further analysis will dichotomize this variable.

These differences in the distribution of ties attenuate slightly when nativity is accounted for. Among three groups, the foreign-born are more like than the natives to lack any ties. The foreign-born black population is small but appears to have as many if not more ties than the native-born black population. Among whites, nativity makes little difference, whereas it matters considerably for the Mexicans and the Chinese. Among the Mexican-origin population, those without ties drop from nearly 43 percent among the foreign-born to 29 percent among the native-born.

Independent variables

The independent variables, all individual-level, examine the effect of demographic characteristics, length of residency in the area, and human capital. The independent variable of most interest is migration status, measured dichotomously as first-generation or later generations. From these data, it would be impossible to distinguish second-generation immigrants from later generations.

Other important demographic characteristics are sex and age. Gender affects the structure and composition of networks (Moore 1990, Wellman and Frank 2001), and international migration in particular can lead to profound shifts in gender relations and the structure of men's and women's networks (Levitt 2001, Menjívar 2000). A measurement of age is important because the networks of older people shrink in size and level of support (Fischer

1982). Even though spouses consistently rank as the strongest social tie (Burt 1986), I do not control for the presence of a spouse because of potential endogeneity. The literature is inconclusive on this point. Some argue that networks tend to affect conjugal relations rather than the other way around (Bott 1955, Milardo and Allan 2000). Others have found that dating and marriage reduce the size of friendship networks (Kalmijn 2003).

Length of residency refers to years in greater Los Angeles, not simply in the United States, since even internal migrants must renegotiate ties at a new destination. It is coded continuously but topcoded at 30 years. Native Angelenos are given a length of residency equal to their age. Because length of residency is not normally distributed, the variable is logged in regression analyses.

Human capital is indicated through education and annual family income. The education variable is dichotomous, since high school graduation represents the threshold credential for entrée into much of the labor market and schooling itself structures the formation of youthful networks. The income variable is represented in thousands of dollars and is logged. Missing data are imputed to the mean, and a dummy variable is used to account for them. Table 3.3 shows the distribution of the marginal totals for the Mexican-origin, Chinese and non-Hispanic blacks and whites in Los Angeles County. All results are weighted using Stata's survey-design module to account for the multi-stage selection process. For more information on these variables, see Appendix C.

Among all residents of Los Angeles County, about 40 percent are foreign-born (see Table 3.1), but the proportions vary widely. More than 95 percent of the Chinese were born abroad, making the native-born generations quite small. Two-thirds of the Mexican-origin sample was born in Mexico. Among other Hispanics, such as Guatemalans or Salvadorans, virtually all were born abroad. By contrast, among non-Hispanic whites, only 16 percent were. They came from a cross-section of countries, the most frequently cited of which were Iran, England, and India. The number of foreign-born blacks is small. A plurality comes from Central America (e.g. Belize), with others from Jamaica, Trinidad and Tobago, and Africa.

Table 3.3   Totals for independent variables among adults in Los Angeles County, by racial and ethnic group

| | Racial/Ethnic Group | | | |
Mexican	Chinese	Non-Hispanic Black	Non-Hispanic White	Total
Percent female				
48.4	46.7	50.7	50.6	50.3
Mean age of adult (age 21+) population				
37.0	45.6	41.2	45.0	41.6
Mean years since arrival in LA area among foreign-born				
13.0	9.9	7.6	18.9	13.4
Percent with high school diploma				
48.1	76.6	88.6	95.4	77.5
Mean family income				
$31,596	$41,548	$41,512	$59,278	$45,580
Percent missing on income variable				
14.0	27.9	12.9	9.0	12.1
Total N				
697	532	1,118	861	4,025

Marked group differences appear in age, as Table 3.3 shows. The mean age of the respondents (all of whom are at least 21) is 37.0 for the Mexicans but at least 45 for the Chinese and non-Hispanic whites, with blacks about halfway between. The mean age of the foreign-born among these groups is approximately the same as for the whole population: 36.0 for the Mexicans, 45.9 for the Chinese and 44.7 for the non-Hispanic whites. The relative youth of the foreign-born Mexican population appears to be explained in part by the average age of arrival: 23.0 for Mexicans, as compared with 36.0 for Chinese. While the majority of both Chinese and Mexicans come at young ages, the age of arrival for Chinese is much more broadly distributed. Nearly 42 percent of Chinese arrived in Los Angeles after the age of 40, whereas only 5.3 percent of the Mexican population did. Because so many Chinese immigrants arrived at older ages, on average, they have not spent as much time in Los Angeles as immigrants from the other groups. For Chinese immigrants, the average time in Los Angeles was not quite 10 years, whereas it was 13.0 years for Mexican immigrants and 18.9 years for non-Hispanic white immigrants. Yet black immigrants are the most recent of all arrivals, at 7.6 years on average.

Status differences are marked. Less than half of the Mexican-origin respondents had high school diplomas, and their mean family income was less than $32,000 a year. More than three-quarters of the Chinese had diplomas, and their mean income was about $10,000 higher. Blacks' mean income was almost identical to that of Chinese, and 88 percent had high school diplomas. Among whites, more than 95 percent had diplomas, and at $59,278, their mean income was nearly twice that of the Mexicans. However, among the Mexicans and Chinese, the differences are strongest among the foreign-born. Only 30 percent of the Mexican-born had a high school diploma, whereas 84 percent of the native-born Mexican-Americans did. Nearly all the native-born Chinese had a diploma, and the native-born Chinese had much higher family incomes than the

Chinese immigrants, though still not so high as the incomes of the whites. However, there was virtually no difference in education levels among foreign-born and native-born whites, and the foreign-born whites had an average annual family income of $73,800 – higher than the native-born.

Findings

To examine what characteristics of immigrants may explain why they have fewer strong ties than the native-born, Table 3.4 regresses the presence of any strong ties on nativity and several other potentially relevant factors: recent arrival in the area, demographic traits, and socioeconomic status.

Model 1 confirms the findings of the previous table, that foreign-born Mexicans are significantly less likely to have strong ties outside the household than native-born Mexican-Americans. However, foreign-born blacks are significantly more likely to report having strong ties. The difference for whites is not significant.

Model 2 examines how the sex and age of respondents is associated with the presence of strong ties. For all groups, women are more likely to have strong ties than men, and the difference is significant for those of Mexican origin. This finding is consistent with the literature on women as the keeper of kinship ties. The effect of age is negligible for Mexicans and blacks but negative for whites. Overall, these two demographic traits do not explain why immigrants have fewer strong ties than the native-born.

Model 3 considers whether years of residence in the city explains the difference in strong ties between immigrants and natives. The positive coefficients for Mexicans and non-Hispanic whites show that recent arrivals are less likely to report strong ties. Moreover, for Mexicans, length of residence reduces the disadvantage that immigrants have in making strong ties. This finding lends

Table 3.4   Logistic regression for presence of strong ties outside the household among Angelenos, by race/ethnicity, nativity, sex, age, length of residence, and socioeconomic status

	Model 1	Model 2	Model 3	Model 4
Mexican-origin				
Foreign-born	-.5971*	-.6298*	-.5089†	-.2213
Female		.4523*	.4525*	.5561**
Age		.0048	.0022	.0080
Years residence, logged			.1357	.0530
High school graduate				.5726*
Family income, logged				.2935
Missing income				-1.1906**
F	4.81*	4.96**	3.98**	5.22**
Non-Hispanic Black				
Foreign-born	1.4415*	1.3724*	1.2127*	.8232
Female		.0934	.1059	.2168
Age		-.0130	-.0121	-.0095
Years residence, logged			-.1430	-.0728
High school graduate				.6230
Family income, logged				.3861*
Missing income				-.6873
F	5.49*	2.56†	2.03†	3.11**
Non-Hispanic White				
Foreign-born	-.3714	-.4434	-.4946	-.5466
Female		.5216	.4359	.5825*
Age		-.0218*	-.0255**	.0202†
Years residence, logged			.0402	-.0109
High school graduate				.4513
Family income, logged				.4232**
Missing income				-1.0189**
F	0.88	3.16*	2.28†	5.14**

† $p<.10$ * $p<.05$ ** $p<.01$

some support to the networks hypothesis. However, among blacks, years of residence works in an unexpected direction: The longer the residence, the less the likelihood of strong ties (though not significantly so). This finding probably reflects the greater level of human capital among internal more than international migrants.

Model 4 takes into account the effect of socioeconomic status on the presence of strong ties outside the household. In all cases, either education or income is significant. Higher socioeconomic status is related to greater probability of strong ties outside the household. For the Mexicans, education matters more than income. For blacks and whites, income matters more than the diploma. The dummy variable for missing income is also significant for Mexicans and whites; those who refused to state their income were also less likely to report strong ties. The variables for socioeconomic status attenuate the effect of nativity among both Mexican-Americans and blacks, suggesting that human capital has notable effects on social ties. Among whites, too, the addition of socioeconomic characteristics also magnifies the disadvantage of foreign birth, because the foreign-born whites earned on average more than the native-born.

Table 3.5 shows the predicted probabilities of strong ties for native-born and foreign-born whites and Mexicans at age 40 with average family income, by both years of residence and socioeconomic status. With both years of residence and socioeconomic status controlled, the effect of foreign birth on the probability of having strong ties outside the household is relatively small for Mexicans and non-Hispanic whites. Blacks are not shown because of the relatively small size of the foreign-born population.

Time in the Los Angeles area makes only a slight difference for those of Mexican origin and none for whites. The effect of at least a high school education has a noticeable effect on the probability of strong ties for all

groups, but especially so for the Mexicans. For Mexican
newcomers, a high school education increases the predicted
probability by roughly 14 percentage points. For whites, a
high school education adds about six percentage points to
the probability.

Table 3.5	Predicted probabilities for the presence of any strong ties among 40-year-old Angelenos, by racial/ethnic group, nativity, education, sex and years of residence

			Years of residence			
			One		Fifteen	
Race/ ethnicity	Nativity	Education	Sex			
			M	F	M	F
Mexican	Native-born	< High school	.57	.67	.60	.72
		H.S. graduate	.70	.80	.72	.82
	Foreign-born	< High school	.51	.65	.55	.68
		H.S. graduate	.65	.76	.68	.79
Non-Hispanic white	Native-born	< High school	.85	.91	.85	.91
		H.S. graduate	.90	.94	.89	.94
	Foreign-born	< High school	.77	.86	.76	.85
		H.S. graduate	.84	.90	.84	.90

Discussion

Both within-group and between-group differences emerge
as important findings. The first key finding is the wide
racial and ethnic disparity in the level of strong ties outside
the household among non-Hispanic whites, Mexicans and
blacks; whites by far report having the most ties. The
second key finding is often large difference between the
foreign-born and native-born of each group in the
proportion with strong ties outside the household.

Native non-Hispanic whites appear to be much more integrated than any other group, with more than 90 percent reporting strong ties outside their households. Even with length of residence and socioeconomic status held constant, whites maintain their advantage over native-born blacks and Mexican-Americans. The question is what accounts for this advantage. To say that it is sheer group size seems unlikely. For one thing, that assumes that non-Hispanic whites are a unified group with one pan-ethnic identity. For another, in Los Angeles County, non-Hispanic whites do not comprise a majority of the population. It is possible native-born whites have an inherent advantage because of generation, in that many of them are third- or even later generation immigrants, whereas many of the native-born Mexicans are only second generation. The effect of second vs. later generations could not be tested with these data. Most likely, however, is that even newly arrived whites find themselves in a structural context that is rich in networks and thus potential friends. Native-born blacks and Mexicans are not likely to be able to tap into co-ethnic networks with that much depth.

Nevertheless, the Mexicans appear to be slowly converging with whites in the likelihood of having strong ties outside the household. Whites get no advantage from living in Los Angeles a long time. Mexicans' networks grow slowly, though after 15 years, Mexicans still do not report the same level of strong ties as whites.

As for the specific hypotheses tested in this paper, the network perspective receives mixed support. Mexican immigrants do not have nearly the same level of strong ties as the natives, despite what a networks perspective might predict. If these immigrants are drawn to Los Angeles by their networks, these networks are still not so large as the networks of the native-born. The exception is the non-

Hispanic whites, whose levels of strong ties are nearly as high as those of native-born whites. For these groups, the positive coefficients for years of residence suggest that immigrants do indeed have to renegotiate their network attachments at the destination. For Mexicans, *growth* in the level of strong ties over time shows that immigrants become embedded, as predicted by the second hypothesis. Black and white immigrants, however, do not become more embedded over time.

Of course, it is possible that more immigrants than reported remain isolated. These would have been more likely to return home and so be omitted from the sample. It is also worth noting that immigrant migration networks need not consist solely of strong ties. Weaker ties that would not show up in this study because of its conservative assumptions might still be strong enough to give potential migrants enough confidence to embark on a transnational trip. Nonetheless, the idea that immigrant networks are solidified by the shared experience of migration seems like a romanticized notion, with no support.

However, the adversity perspective also gets only qualified support. As the first hypothesis predicted, lower socioeconomic levels among immigrants are associated with fewer strong ties. But immigrant whites, who generally have *high* socioeconomic levels, also report fewer strong ties than the native-born, so low status and competition among immigrants alone do not fully explain immigrants' lower number of strong ties. In fact, in some cases the effect of status is counterintuitive. The addition of socioeconomic variables to the regression analysis in Table 4 not only fails to explain why immigrant whites have fewer strong ties than the native-born of the same groups, these SES variables *magnify* the differences between the native-born and foreign-born. Only for the Mexicans do

SES variables work as expected, to attenuate the effect of foreign birth.

Overall, the two perspectives work differently for the various groups. For Mexicans, both the networks perspective and the socioeconomic perspective explain part of the difference in the level of strong ties between the native-born and the foreign-born. Together, the two perspectives largely attenuate the negative effect of foreign birth. For non-Hispanic whites, any change in the probability of strong ties is small, since even newly arrived immigrants report high levels of strong ties. For whites, years of residence have no effect at all. Yet this surprising finding suggests that immigrant and migrant whites may be the ones with the most ready-made networks of all; with their high income, those whites who migrate to Los Angeles appear to be self-selected for their human capital and social capital. For whites, family income increases the probability of strong ties, but since immigrant whites earn on average more than the native-born, increased SES does not attenuate but in fact increases the difference between the native-born and foreign-born. Whites appear most likely to arrive with networks intact, in line with the transnational migration perspective.

For all these group variations, it remains that immigrants generally report fewer strong ties than the native-born. This lack of ties among the immigrant generation may be a transitory phenomenon. The obvious relationship between education and strong ties suggests that greater access to schooling will increase the chances of forming strong ties. As the numbers of the native-born generation grow, they will probably reap the advantages of larger group size and gain access to more diverse networks. As native-born Americans, they will also share a language and much of the same culture as all other Americans, and this exposure to a shared culture is likely to promote more intergroup ties.

So then, is a lack of social ties a problem? Certainly, it is in the short run. First-generation immigrants have never been expected on a large scale to surmount language and cultural barriers. If they have fewer friends or kin from whom to draw social support, they may be more subject to stress and other ailments whose effects are buffered by emotional support. Fewer social ties could also be a problem in the long run. Social support from the broader immigrant community is often critical to the success of immigrant children (Zhou and Bankston 1998). If the parents of the second generation have neither their own resources nor connections to the broader community, their children face greater risk of downward mobility (Portes and Rumbaut 2001). While the results are not generalizable beyond Los Angeles, the similarities in networks between the varying groups that have settled in Los Angeles suggest patterns that might appear in other cities as well. If so, isolation among the first generation could be a widespread phenomenon.

CHAPTER 4
Kinship Ties

The previous chapter showed that the native-born report significantly more strong ties outside their households than immigrants. This chapter examines the composition of those strong ties, whether they are with kin or friends. The chapter also looks at whether immigration (or, more broadly, migration) influences the kinds of strong ties that people form. Of course, the analysis in this chapter can reflect the characteristics of *only* those who have reported strong ties. As shown in the previous chapter, these respondents constitute three-quarters of the sample from Los Angeles.

The difference between kin and non-kin

The distinction between kin and non-kin is fundamental to the division of the social network (Adams 1967, Fischer 1982: 80). We can pick our neighbors, to the extent that income and other social constraints allow us mobility. We can pick our co-workers, to some degree, in that we have some choice of occupation and job and thus the type of people with whom we work. We can pick our friends, subject to constraints of time and the availability of persons with sufficiently common interests. But we cannot pick our kin. The only choice regarding kin is how (and how often) we interact with them. (One must note, however, that fictive or pseudo-kinship can blur the distinction between kin and non-kin, e.g. Liebow 1967 and Stack 1974.) Moreover, kinship ties are permanent, whereas other types of ties can be dropped.

Basically, kin and non-kin serve different functions. Kin provide help in crises, as well as social and instrumental support (Litwak and Szelenyi 1969). Kinship ties can be neglected for a while without withering, though not indefinitely (Fischer 1982), and maintenance of these ties still often depends upon the ability of family members to engage in reciprocal exchanges (Menjívar 2000). Friends provide greater companionship along the life course, but friendships may be specific to a place and time and thus wax and wane according to the life cycle (Fischer et al. 1977). Even so, the most frequent get-togethers are with kin (Axelrod 1956). Reliance solely on friends rather than kin may indicate a weaker safety net in the event of a personal crisis, in that kin are more likely than friends to provide instrumental aid. Reliance solely on kin rather than friendships may restrict some opportunities for information and any social or economic advantages ensuing from that information.

As in Chapter 3, the perspectives of social networks and adversity lead to diverging expectations on the type of strong ties that people will maintain. The networks approach examines the structural underpinnings for potential ties. The constraints on ties are dual: proximity, or the opportunity to forge strong ties, and homophily, or the tendency to choose associates similar to oneself. The ability to develop strong ties is thus tempered mainly by the availability of similar people (Blau 1977). The adversity perspective stresses socioeconomic limitations on the ability to develop and maintain strong ties. Maintaining strong ties requires time, access to others, social skills, and often enough resources to engage in reciprocal exchanges. Those with low socioeconomic status would be less likely to be able to maintain strong ties. This would be true in particular for friendships, which are not determined by birth but by choice, but also for those living beyond the neighborhood, so that some effort is required to maintain contact. These different emphases lead to differing, testable hypotheses.

Social networks. Strong ties thrive on face-to-face interaction (Homans 1950). So, having kin nearby should result in a greater likelihood of seeing one another and retaining strong kinship ties. People living in the area where they were born ("hometowners") almost by definition have or have had some kin nearby, by virtue of the families in which they grew up. Naturally, migrants to the city could have kin nearby, too, but the very act of migration means that these respondents moved away from kin at some point. In the case of immigrants, the kin left behind are in another country, so that maintaining interactions is even more difficult. Therefore, net of other characteristics, adults living in the region of their birth should have more potential kinship ties than those who have migrated.

Adversity. From the adversity perspective, income and other socioeconomic characteristics matter. The lower the respondent's level of resources, the more difficulty the respondent will have in maintaining ties. Therefore, respondents with lower socioeconomic status, if they have ties at all, should have the easier types of ties to maintain. These would be with kin – relations with whom are determined by birth – and with those who are close by. Lower socioeconomic status should be associated with more kinship ties than friend ties because of the difficulty of forging and maintaining friendships with few resources.

Table 4.1   Proportion of respondent-alter strong ties by relationship and alter (standard errors in parentheses)[1]

	Alter 1	Alter 2	Alter 3	All[2]
Relative	.242	.268	.259	.253
	(.016)	(.0 17)	(.019)	(.013)
Friend	.546	.526	.550	.546
	(.020)	(.019)	(.020)	(.015)
Co-worker	.073	.087	.078	.076
	(.010)	(.012)	(.014)	(.009)
Other	.140	.120	.112	.124
	(.013)	(.013)	(.013)	(.010)
Total N	2,309	1,995	1,604	2,309

1. Answers are based on the question "What is person 1's [or 2's or 3's] relationship to you?" This question was asked only of respondents who named at least one person in response to a name-generator question.
2. Overall proportion is based on the number of respondents, not the number of respondent-alter pairs.

Findings

The most commonplace tie among confidants is that of friendship (see Table 4.1). Nearly 55 percent of all discussion partners are friends of the respondents. This relationship, if anything, may be understated, since respondents were given a list of types of relationships and asked to choose one. A co-worker listed as a discussion partner may also be a friend as well as fill another role. This ambiguity in roles related to friendship suggests that the major conceptual break lies between kin and non-kin, and the rest of this chapter will be based on this distinction.

Table 4.1 also shows that as discussion partners, relatives come far behind friends. Only one-quarter of all discussion partners have kinship ties to the respondents. This pattern holds across alters, suggesting that in these data, the order in which alters are listed is not meaningful.

Table 4.2   Proportion of ties by type, by race/ethnicity (standard errors in parentheses)

	No kin ties	Kin and non-kin ties	Only kin ties	Total
N-H Black	.488	.385	.136	1.00
	(.046)	(.050)	(.023)	
Hispanic	.596	.289	.114	1.00
	(.029)	(.025)	(.017)	
Asian	.561	.263	.176	1.00
	(.062)	(.054)	(.050)	
N-H white	.569	.342	.089	1.00
	(.024)	(.023)	(.015)	
All	.565	.329	.106	1.00
	(.018)	(.017)	(.011)	

Since three-fourths of all ties are not with kin, one might expect that a large proportion of respondents would report that *all* of their discussion partners were also unrelated to them. In fact, this is the case (see Table 4.2). Table 4.2 divides the array of ties that respondents report into three categories: non-kin only, kin and non-kin, and kin only. The table further disaggregates the data by the race/ethnicity of the respondent. The proportions describe the set of ties reported by each respondent, and the survey weights are therefore those of the respondent and are not based on respondent-alter dyads.

Overall, 56.5 percent of respondents report that their alters contain no kin, and 10.6 percent that their alters comprise only kin. The remaining third report both kinds of ties. Distinct racial and ethnic variations emerge. Kinship ties are most commonplace among non-Hispanic blacks. More than half of those who report ties have some with kin. Kinship ties are least commonplace among Hispanics, with 60 percent reporting no confidants among relatives, despite cultural emphasis on the family. This surprising finding may be explained by the availability of kin and will be tested later in this chapter. Non-Hispanic whites are nearly as likely to report no kinship ties at all, and they are the least likely group to report ties exclusively with family.

Table 4.3   Proportion of respondents whose alters are exclusively kin, by number of alters (standard errors in parentheses)

Number of alters	One	Two	Three	Total
	.241	.111	.068	.091
	(.051)	(.023)	(.010)	(.010)
N	313	391	1,605	2,309

The rest of this chapter focuses on networks that are exclusively with kin. Exclusivity of kinship ties is theoretically interesting in that it represents a clear choice among alternatives. One may not have any relatives nearby, but potential friends abound. Moreover, while kin-only networks may be highly supportive, they are least likely to contain any bridges to other groups or to foster integration into a larger culture. Among those whose ties are only with kin, 8.7 percent overall report that one of those alters is a different race or ethnicity. Among respondents with non-kin in their networks, 31.8 percent report an alter of a different race. One might ask whether network size accounts for the difference, since those with smaller networks are more likely to report them as exclusively with kin. (See Table 4.3.) But even among those with three kin as alters, the proportion with racial/ethnic bridge ties stands at only 13.6 percent. Furthermore, as Table 4.3 shows, respondents who report having alters are likeliest to report the full three.

Of course, the ability to maintain any strong ties with kin may hinge on the presence of kin, so it becomes important to distinguish not only immigrants but also internal migrants from native Angelenos. Almost by definition, hometowners have kin in the area. Among these natives who report social ties, slightly more than 13 percent say that their strong ties are exclusively with kin. By comparison, 7 percent of those who migrated to Los Angeles have strong ties exclusively with kin.

Table 4.4 presents a logistic regression for strong ties exclusively with kin. As Model 1 shows, even with other demographic and background characteristics controlled, minorities are significantly more likely than non-Hispanic whites to report their alters as exclusively kin. Although women have generally been found to keep up family relationships (e.g. Roschelle 1997), they are no more likely than men to have social networks *exclusively* with family. However, a separate regression (not shown) shows that women are significantly more likely than men to have *some* kin in their social networks.

The household composition is important to determining whether social ties are exclusively with kin. When other adults live in the household, the likelihood of networks composed entirely of kin goes down. Most likely, the adults in the household are immediate kin, so strong ties with them may well exist but would not be captured by a question that specifically asks for discussants outside the household. The presence of a spouse increases the likelihood of kin-only ties, not only because in-laws increase the pool of kin who could become confidants, but also because marriage can disrupt friendship patterns. The presence of children also makes couples more family-oriented.

Table 4.4   Logistic coefficients for strong ties exclusively with kin, by race/ethnicity, family characteristics, background and socioeconomic status

	Model 1	Model 2
Number of alters	-.6928***	-.7053***
Black	.6045*	.6388*
Hispanic	.6364*	.6313*
Asian	1.0033*	1.0372*
Female	.0841	.1258
No. other adults in household	-.4112**	-.4209**
Presence of spouse or partner	.5909*	.5606*
Own children <18 in household	.3589	.2828
Age 65+	1.367***	1.4893***
Native of city	.7253**	.7195**
Foreign-born	-.0318	.0140
In the workforce		.2071
Did not finish high school		-.1904
Family income, logged		.0773
Dummy for missing income		-.1679
F	9.51***	7.81***

*p<.05 **p<.01 ***p<.001

Native Angelenos are also twice as likely to have ties exclusively with kin than are migrants to the city. Migrants may not have kin in the area, whereas the natives would often have family around. U.S.-born migrants to the city are no more or less likely than immigrants to report social ties exclusively with kin. The key difference, as expected, is growing up in the city.

Age also has a remarkable effect on the composition of networks. People age 65 and up are nearly four times as likely as working-age people to say their alters are only kin. The effect is not linear, but more of a threshold one that appears after retirement age. This threshold makes conceptual sense in light of previous research on men showing that the working ages form a natural boundary for friendships (Fischer et al. 1977).

The addition of socioeconomic variables does not explain the composition of social ties. The education variable runs in the expected direction, but not strongly, showing that people without a high school diploma are more likely to have ties only with family. However, presence in the workforce also increases the tendency toward kin-only ties, though again, not strongly. The weak explanatory power of these variables suggests that an adversity or inequality perspective is not relevant to an understanding of the composition of social networks.

Instead, the results suggest that a family orientation, suggested through marriage and children, as well as the presence of kin in the area, is much more likely to explain why some respondents report only kin among their social ties. Immigrants and internal migrants find themselves in the similar situations of having fewer kin available in the area than those who grew up in Los Angeles. All these factors support the networks perspective,

However, what remains are strong racial and ethnic differences not accounted for by socioeconomic status or household composition. Blacks and Hispanics (and Asians, insofar as the data are trustworthy) have fewer ties overall than non-Hispanic whites. And the networks that they describe have more ties exclusively with kin. As a buffer, these kin-only relationship may work well. But insofar as these respondents need bridge ties to realize more opportunities, the findings suggest that minority groups may have more difficulty using these ties for information.

CHAPTER 5
Ties with Neighbors

The distinction between neighborhood strong ties and more distant ties has been central to the study of sociology. "Proximity and neighborly contact are the basis for the simplest and most elementary form of association," wrote Robert Park in 1916 (Park 1969: 96) in one of the seminal essays of the Chicago School. Nor has modern technology fundamentally changed that basis of association. Because neighboring depends upon proximity, ties among neighbors generally cut across different dimensions than ties between kin and non-kin. People pick their neighbors indirectly through their choice of neighborhood, though the extent of such choice is limited by income, availability of information and potential discrimination. This means that neighbors are more likely to be similar in class, race and religion than the city as a whole. Within neighborhoods, people can choose their relationships with their neighbors, keeping them as "just neighbors" or forging a social group of "real neighbors" (Fischer 1984: 131). If a neighbor becomes a friend, the role of the neighbor changes. Otherwise, the role ends when a neighbor moves.

Views of the role of urban neighboring vary. One is a minimalist, "residual" view of neighboring, prevalent particularly in poorer communities, in which neighbors provide mainly emergency assistance and mutual aid but little social interaction beyond a diffuse friendliness (Keller 1968, Hunter 1978). Another view of neighboring holds that attachment to community is limited (hence the term "community of limited liability") but varies by social roles. The nature of the social role depends upon the neighborhood social structure, such as the density of settlement, the economic status of the residents and the level of cooperation and trust among residents. (Greer 1962, Keller 1968: 26). A third view of neighboring is that it competes with potential ties beyond the neighborhood. People seek out those like them; those with more options would have a broader range of choice and would be more likely to go beyond the neighborhood. Neighborhood ties are then strongest among people with impeded access to distant ties, such as children, the infirm and those lacking access to a car or public transportation. The neighborhood also retains an advantage when one's kin live there or when residents unite to fulfill local needs (Fischer 1984: 132-133, Logan and Spitze 1994). A fourth view holds that the neighborhood is integrated into a broader system rather than operating as a distinct entity in its own right – that is, the concept of neighborhood has no clear spatial boundaries. "The local community is viewed as a complex system of friendship and kinship networks and formal and informal associational ties rooted in family life and on-going socialization processes" (Kasarda and Janowitz 1974: 329.) These four views are not mutually exclusive.

The assumptions underlying this chapter fall between the third and fourth views. By contrasting ties between neighbors and others more distant, this analysis implies that strong ties with neighbors are potentially substantively different from strong ties with others. Such an argument, similar to the third view above, extends the work of Bott (1955), who found that differential types of networks shaped conjugal relations. The shaping of family relations would most likely take place when *all* reported strong ties are with neighbors, rather than a mixture of ties inside and outside the neighborhood. Strong ties exclusively with neighbors, reminiscent of the "community saved," would indicate informal social control and ecological sorting (Wellman 1979). At the same time, this analysis also acknowledges that social networks are formed within a larger integrated system, reminiscent of the fourth view above.

However, drawing a distinction between neighbors and non-neighbors presents the traditional problem of defining a neighborhood. Research on the meaning of neighborhood is inconclusive. Some neighborly relations are specific to the facing block (Greenbaum and Greenbaum 1985), and some to a network of residential streets (Grannis 1998). One study found that the territorial definition of "neighborhood" averaged 15 blocks but also reported wide deviation from that mean (Lee and Campbell 1997). Many surveys leave the definition of "neighborhood" up to the respondent. Census-based studies are forced to choose one of the census units (the tract, block group, or block) as a proxy for neighborhood. In the MCSUI, the definition of ethnic concentration, neighborhood status and neighbor come from different sources. The concentration is determined by the racial composition of the respondent's census tract and the neighborhood status by the characteristics of the respondent's block group. The respondents themselves decide whether someone else lives in the same neighborhood.[2]

Networks and adversity perspectives

As in Chapter 4, the perspectives of social networks and poverty lead to different though not mutually exclusive expectations on the spatial location of the discussion partners named by respondents.

Social networks. Because of the importance of face-to-face interaction in maintaining strong ties (Homans 1950), neighbors become obvious candidates for such ties by dint of their proximity. But proximity is hardly enough for strong ties to form. Not everyone sees the neighbors, let alone socializes with them. For someone living nearby to go from "just a neighbor" to a strong tie, other bases for social ties have to be present. The most common such basis is homophily, whether the commonality is ethnicity, gender, age, family status, religion, or something more particularistic, like interest in soccer. Residence among co-ethnics, particularly in an enclave or at least among a concentration of co-ethnics, should provide greater availability of similar people for potential strong ties.

Adversity. From a perspective of adversity, income and other socioeconomic characteristics should affect the spatial distribution of network ties, but both at an individual and contextual level. Neighborhood poverty should undermine the ability of an area to maintain the kinds of institutions that bring people together and encourage long-term settlement. As a result, one would expect to find fewer

---

[2] Questions about neighborhood were asked only of those respondents who gave a first name or initials in response to the name-generator question. MCSUI's neighborhood question is "Does person 1 [or 2 or 3] live in your neighborhood?"

ties with neighbors in poorer neighborhoods. At the individual level, intervening opportunities also matter. People outside the workforce may stay mainly in their own neighborhoods and therefore may have more neighborhood ties than those who are employed. Lower family income may also make it hard to sustain more distant ties, so poorer families would also be more likely to rely on neighbors for their strong ties.

Findings

Local community ties remain highly salient in Los Angeles. Near 38 percent of the strong ties reported were with people who live in respondents' neighborhoods. Moreover, the first person named by a respondent was more likely to be a neighbor than the second or third person, as shown by Table 5.1. Among alters listed first, more than 41 percent are neighbors of the respondent. This difference suggests that to the extent that people list their closest ties first, proximity matters considerably. However, it is important not to draw a causal inference, since some respondents may have drawn close to their neighbors, while others may have chosen their neighborhoods on the basis on who lived there.

Table 5.2 shows the proportion of respondents whose strong ties are exclusively with neighbors. Such ties are important because they symbolize respondents whose strongest ties appear to be bounded by the local community. Such ties are the individual-level counterparts of the Wellman's conception of the "community saved." In all, 22.2 percent of respondents report ties only within the neighborhood. In this case, the number of alters is crucial. If one arbitrarily considers the probability of any alter living in the same neighborhood as .5, the probability of having two alters in the neighborhood is .25 and three is

.125. In fact, 47.3 percent of those respondents with only one alter did say that the alter lived in the neighborhood. Among respondents with three alters, 16.1 percent reported that all three lived in the neighborhood.

Table 5.1   Proportion of respondent-alter strong ties that are with neighbors, by alter (standard errors in parentheses)[1]

	Alter 1	Alter 2	Alter 3	All[2]
	.412	.369	.323	.379
	(.019)	(.017)	(.019)	(.015)
N	2,308	1,997	1,608	2,310

1. Answers are based on the question "Does person 1 [or 2 or 3] live in your neighborhood?" This question was asked only of respondents who named at least one person in response to a name-generator question. The question was repeated up to three times, depending on how many alters the respondent had named. (For more details on the name-generator, see Appendix B.)
2. Overall proportion is based on the number of respondents, not the number of respondent-alter pairs. The total is two greater than the number of first alters because of two missing cases in responses to the question on the first alter: "Does person 1 live in your neighborhood?"

Table 5.3 further compares the proportion of networks that are exclusively within the neighborhood to networks that have no neighbors and networks with both neighbors and more distal alters. Ties with people beyond the neighborhood – analogous to Wellman's "community liberated" – comprise 43.2 percent of all networks, or almost twice the level of neighborhood-only ties. More than a third of the networks consist of ties both inside and outside the neighborhood. Presumably, if respondents were able to list more alters, the proportion of networks in the category would grow.

The proportion of respondents with these types of ties varies widely by racial and ethnic group. More than half of black and Asian respondents reported that their networks contained no neighbors; for Hispanics, slightly more than a third contained no neighbors. On the other hand, Hispanics as a group report that nearly 30 percent of their networks are *exclusively* with neighbors, almost twice the rate of blacks. Asians and non-Hispanic whites fall in between, at just under 20 percent of their networks being only with neighbors. The Asian sample, of course, may suffer from some selection bias, since the proportion of respondents with ties at all appears to be underestimated. Potential bias notwithstanding, the Asians tend to live amid far fewer co-ethnics than the other groups. The size of their population in Los Angeles County is much smaller than that of non-Hispanic whites and Hispanics. And unlike blacks, their segregation from non-Hispanic whites tends to be only moderate. As a result, the average Asian neighborhood has far fewer co-ethnic Asians to be potential discussion partners than the average neighborhood of whites, blacks or Hispanics.

Table 5.2   Proportion of Respondents Whose Strong Ties Are Exclusively With Neighbors, by Number of Alters

Number of Alters	One	Two	Three	Total Alters
	.473	.294	.161	.222
	(.065)	(.039)	(.014)	(.014)
N	313	391	1,606	2,310

Unclear still is the extent to which these racial and ethnic differences stem from contextual factors such as co-ethnic concentration or poverty or from individual-level characteristics, such as length in the neighborhood. Particularly when much of the literature on ethnic enclaves stresses their cohesiveness, it becomes important to determine whether groups whose members tend to be immigrants or their children benefit greater social ties within the neighborhood.

Table 5.3   Proportion of ties by neighborhood location, by race/ethnicity (standard errors in parentheses)

	No ties with neighbors	Ties with neighbors and others	Ties only with neighbors	Total
N-H Black	.538 (.042)	.310 (.036)	.152 (.027)	1.00
Hispanic	.356 (.032)	.346 (.028)	.298 (.027)	1.00
Asian	.608 (.056)	.199 (.036)	.193 (.044)	1.00
N-H white	.441 (.029)	.360 (.026)	.199 (.019)	1.00
All	.432 (.019)	.343 (.0180)	.222 (.014)	1.00

Table 5.4 offers a multinomial analysis comparing the characteristics of respondents whose social networks are exclusively distal, exclusively neighborhood-based, or a combination of the two. Each model in the weighted regression includes the number of alters, since a greater number of alters increases the likelihood that any respondent will have ties both inside and beyond the neighborhood.

Model 1 considers only the contextual variables. Living amid many co-ethnics is associated significantly with more ties with neighbors. This supports the expectation that people seek homophilous ties. At the same time, the adversity perspective is also supported. People in poor neighborhoods are less likely to have ties with neighbors, especially ties exclusively with neighbors, than they are to have ties beyond the neighborhood.

Table 5.4 Multinomial regression for strong ties with neighbors, by structure of ties, neighborhood context, demographic traits, and socioeconomic status

	Model 1	Model 2	Model 3	Model 4
Ties both inside and outside neighborhood (Omitted: Only distal ties)				
Number of alters	1.2793***	1.2610***	1.2939***	1.3157***
Outside concentration	-.4535**			-.4133**
Neighborhood status	-.1737			.-.1322
Black		-.1782	-.3196	-.2220
Hispanic		.2144	.0481	.1246
Asian		-.9398**	-.9916**	-.9039**
Female		.3064*	.1738	.1763
Age		-.0022	-.0068	-.0046
Own children < 18		.1887	.2626	.2548
Foreign-born		.1351	.0995	.0912
Years at present address		.0248*	.0282**	.0261**
In the workforce			-.4008*	-.4388*
High school graduate			-.0195	.0769
Family income, logged			-.3001**	-.2353*
Dummy missing income			.3306	.3981
Ties exclusively in neighborhood (Omitted: Distal ties)				
Number of alters	-.3806**	-.4316**	-.3662**	-.3580**
Outside enclave	-.3599*			-.3498
Neighborhood status	-.2284*			-.0306
Black		-.4391	-.6690*	-.5626
Hispanic		.4472	.1186	.2407
Asian		-.5700	-.6129	-.5335
Female		-.0398	-.2150	-.2260
Age		.0271**	.0179*	.0185*
Own children < 18		.7192***	.7614***	.7531***
Foreign-born		.5185*	.3925	.3774
Years at present address		.0131	.0182	.0161
In the workforce			-.5411*	-.5721*
High school graduate			-.3761	-.3229
Family income, logged			-.3833**	-.3644**
Dummy missing income			.3227	.3791
F	15.72***	7.91***	8.18***	7.68***

*p<.05 **p<.01 ***p<.001

Model 2 examines the association between demographic characteristics and the spatial location of social networks. Race/ethnicity, gender, age, life course, length of residence, and nativity are influential. As Table 5.3 showed, Hispanics are the most likely to ties within the neighborhood, even when controlling for foreign birth, though they are not significantly different from the next group, non-Hispanic whites. Compared with those two groups, blacks and Asians are much more likely to report social ties beyond the neighborhood than with neighbors. As for gender, women are significantly more likely than men to have social networks both inside and beyond the neighborhood than only beyond the neighborhood. At the same time, in a comparison of only distant ties to only neighborhood ones, there is hardly any difference between men and women. By contrast, parents are more likely than the childless to have ties exclusively within the neighborhood. This effect is especially pronounced among non-Hispanic whites – a finding that echoes the findings of Sampson, Morenoff and Earls (1999) on the greater levels of social control of children in white neighborhoods. Age also is associated with an increase in neighborhood-only ties, but the effect is more linear than threshold and begins long before retirement age. Unlike age, the number of years spent at the current address affects the presence of *any* neighborhood ties rather than exclusively neighborhood ties. The years at an address may indicate self-selected stayers, who are happy with the neighborhood. Last, immigrants are much more likely to have exclusively neighborbood ties than exclusively distal ties. This tendency may reflect residency in an ethnic enclave or lower socioeconomic status than the native-born.

Model 3 takes into account the socioeconomic variables. Indeed, socioeconomic status does explain much of the effect of foreign birth. Both presence in the workforce and income increase the chances that a social network will be entirely outside the respondent's neighborhood. Employed people are less likely to have neighborhood ties. They can interact with people on the job, and they generally have to leave their neighborhoods to go to work. They also have the resources to maintain ties outside their neighborhoods. This finding generally supports the adversity perspective and shows that resources influence the structure of social ties. Accounting for socioeconomic status also reduces the effect of gender on the location of social networks. However, while socioeconomic status accounts for much of the tendency of Hispanics to hold more social ties within the neighborhood, this is not the case for blacks. Net of employment, blacks are more likely to have social networks beyond their immediate neighborhoods.

In the full model, reintroduction of neighborhood characteristics does not boost overall explanatory power, but neither are all the neighborhood influences diminished. With demographic and socioeconomic characteristics controlled, residence inside a co-ethnic concentration[3] is still more associated with ties in the neighborhood than with no neighborhood ties. Preference for homophilous ties seems to override the proximity of neighbors in determining the structure of social networks. However, socioeconomic status matters more at the individual level than at the neighborhood level. Family income and employment affect the spatial location of social networks more than does the overall poverty in the neighborhood.

Table 5.5 presents the predicted probability of any strong ties in the neighborhood for respondents by

---

[3] I use co-ethnic concentration when possible instead of "enclave" because the term seems inappropriate for non-Hispanic whites.

race/ethnicity, nativity, income, place of residence and city. The overall trend shows some wide variations among groups. The probabilities are highest for Hispanics. For the most part, poor people have a greater proportion of strong ties within the neighborhood than middle-income people. The difference is most notable among native-born blacks in black neighborhoods. This seems to give support to Wilson's (1987) observations on the difficulty of poor blacks being able to forge ties outside the ghetto.

Table 5.5   Predicted probability of strong ties with neighbors, by structure of ties, neighborhood context, demographic traits, and socioeconomic status

	Income level	Co-ethnic neighborhood	Not co-ethnic neighborhood
Non-Hispanic White			
1st generation	$30,000+	.58	.50
	<$15,000	.68	.40
Native-born	$30,000+	.53	.49
	<$15,000	.60	.52
Black			
Native-born	$30,000+	.58	.47
	<$15,000	.64	.52
Hispanic			
1st generation	$30,000+	.67	.56
	<$15,000	.71	.62
Native-born	$30,000+	.60	.44
	<$15,000	.66	.55

For the immigration status, the effects are mixed. Whites and Hispanics in Los Angeles appear to follow what would be considered a classic assimilation pattern. The first generation has greater probabilities of strong ties within a co-ethnic neighborhood than later generations, regardless of income. On the other hand, whites and

Hispanics who are not living among co-ethnics are more likely to have neighborhood ties if they are native-born than immigrant. This would suggest a greater possibility of strong ties with people of other racial or ethnic backgrounds and thus more assimilation. However, this possibility is subject to the ecological fallacy, since strong ties within a neighborhood need not be with members of the racial or ethnic group comprising the majority in that neighborhood. The next chapter will address the level of homophilous ties more directly.

These predicted probabilities give some support to both the networks and poverty perspectives. The greater likelihood of strong neighborhood ties among residents living in concentrations favors a social networks perspective. However, in this perspective, the probabilities should remain the same across income levels, since the co-ethnic concentration itself provides the structure for potential ties and income should not play a factor. Instead, lack of income clearly appears to restrict the ability of many groups to forge strong ties outside the neighborhood. This latter finding is predicted by the poverty perspective and suggests that SES affects the structuring of social networks.

Discussion

Chapter 3 showed that in terms of overall number of strong ties, minorities gained no advantage from living in co-ethnic concentrations. But as this chapter shows, such concentrations also confer the kind advantages that one would expect – at least for those residents who have strong ties. For them, living among co-ethnics increases chances of strong ties with neighbors as opposed to more distant alters.

Socioeconomic status also affects the likelihood of strong ties with neighbors. The poor or jobless are more likely than the employed to have ties exclusively with neighbors. This trend would indicate that the poor have fewer opportunities to get out of the neighborhood. For them, the choice of alters may be the neighbors or no one. This finding bolsters the adversity perspective.

Individual-level characteristics also influence the likelihood of neighborhood ties. Immigrants are more likely to have strong ties within their neighborhood, in keeping with traditional assimilation theory viewing the enclave as a cocoon; however, the relative poverty of the immigrant generation compared with the native-born also accounts for the greater number of neighborhood ties. Parents, too, are more likely to have ties with neighbors. Neighborhood old-timers have more nearby strong ties, though, of course, they may be old-timers because they liked their neighbors and chose to stay. Ethnicity has a distinct effect, with Hispanics appearing to be much more likely to maintain strong ties within the neighborhood.

Among all groups, the percentage of strong ties within the neighborhood approaches at least 30 percent overall. About 20 percent of respondents report only neighbors as their strong ties. This means that a majority of strong ties lie beyond the neighborhood, in other parts of the city or world. This finding is certainly suggestive of the "community liberated," with its far-flung networks. But the proportion of people whose ties are purely local remains substantial. This level of neighborhood involvement, together with the importance of enclaves, suggests considerable support for the continuance of the "community saved" with its dense, localized ties and for the "community mediate" of Guest (2000), where relationships span types of community.

Left unanswered by this chapter are the demographic characteristics of the alters themselves. Chapter 6 will examine the level of homophily among alters. It will look at such questions as whether strong ties with neighbors involve any trade-offs in homophily for proximity and what, if anything, is related to racially heterogeneous ties among immigrants and minorities.

CHAPTER 6
Similarity in Neighborhood Ties

This chapter returns to the larger question of structural assimilation and how it may be reflected in the networks of the foreign-born in comparison to the native-born. Specifically, the chapter examines the extent to which immigrants and the native-born maintain strong ties within their own racial or ethnic groups and the spatial and socioeconomic circumstances under which any heterogeneous ties are formed. Heterogeneity, particularly along racial or ethnic lines, would be a strong indicator of assimilation, since the homophily principle holds that people prefer to interact with those who are most like themselves. Heterogeneous linkages indicate a shortening of the social distance among groups, which is a harbinger of assimilation. No society has completely heterogeneous ties, since that would indicate equal closeness among all groups regardless of ethnicity, sex, gender, education, age and many other dimensions. Given these circumstances, one can argue that assimilation is occurring when a new group's level of intergroup contact approximates the contact level of a reference population.

Blau's theory (1977) on group size and inequality tends to run along slightly contradictory lines for predicting the level of homophily among immigrants. On the one hand,

Blau holds that small groups tend to be more likely to engage in heterogeneous relations. On the other, Blau also argues that in-group relations are cemented through ascriptive dimensions, such as race or gender, and through the presence of complementary parameters. For many immigrants, ethnic, language and cultural barriers constitute just such parameters. For immigrants, relatively small group size would be less important than their distinctiveness. This leads to the hypothesis that in general, immigrants will be more racially or ethnically homophilous in their strong ties than the native-born population.

Neighborhood context influences the development of social networks. People who reside among co-ethnics would be expected to have more homophilous ties, because they would have more contact with co-ethnics. People who are minorities in their neighborhoods would presumably develop more intergroup ties, both because they see other groups and because their place of residence reflects no strong preference for co-ethnics. So long as these people voluntarily chose their place of residence, they could be considered spatially assimilated. But if people who are minorities in their neighborhoods are also immigrants, they may never develop intergroup ties. The addition of cultural and linguistic barriers to racial or ethnic differences may relegate immigrants' neighborhood contacts with members of other groups to the superficial "just neighbors" type that never develops into friendships. Immigrants who can afford middle-class suburbs may maintain what Zelinsky and Lee (1998) call "heterolocal" networks of social ties regardless of neighborhood. These far-flung ties among immigrants suggest a second hypothesis specifying an interaction between nativity and neighborhood on ties: Residence outside a co-ethnic enclave will be associated with fewer homophilous ties among the native-born. Immigrants will have homophilous ties regardless of whether they live in an enclave.

This hypothesis implies that immigrant groups have choice in their housing. Despite well-documented evidence of housing discrimination against blacks and Hispanics (Yinger 1995), an emerging body of work shows that many wealthy or highly skilled immigrants freely choose their place of residence (Tseng 1995; Zelinsky and Lee 1998; Logan et al. 2002). In general, spatial assimilation has long been associated with socioeconomic mobility (Massey and Denton 1987). Because those who can afford richer areas have financial and human capital, they are also likely to have a large and varied network of acquaintances as well, since money and skills often indicate social capital (Portes 1998). This overall variety should also mean more variety among strong ties as well. But again, immigrants would confront more cultural and linguistic barriers than the native-born to interracial or interethnic ties. So the heterogeneous ties assumed to devolve from spatial assimilation should develop mainly among the native-born. Residence in a poor neighborhood as a member of a minority should not be associated with more heterogeneity in social ties, either for the native-born or foreign-born, because the resident presumably has no other choice of neighborhood and would not necessarily have much social capital. So for those native-born who are living outside ethnic enclaves, one would expect a further interaction involving the wealth of the neighborhood: Residence in wealthier areas outside a co-ethnic concentration will be associated with lower levels of homophily than residence in poorer neighborhoods. Immigrants will have highly homophilous ties regardless of the wealth of their neighborhoods.

Unclear is whether strong ties with neighbors are more or less homophilous than ties with people beyond the neighborhood. Strong ties with neighbors are voluntary associations that may involve more closeness than neighboring relations that otherwise end when someone moves. Because these ties emerge from common interests and not just proximity, strong ties with neighbors should be as homophilous as strong ties with more distant alters, regardless of the type of neighborhood. Neighborhood context may determine not the level of homophily in ties, but the proportion of ties that are with neighbors. In poor neighborhoods with high turnover and few solid institutions, strong ties with neighbors may be rarer than in more stable areas, regardless of the ethnic mix. On the other hand, poor immigrants may be more place-bound than natives and thus rely on co-ethnic neighborhoods for their social support. These two tendencies need not be contradictory, because they cross two dimensions. Therefore, one can expect that the level of homophily in strong ties will be roughly the same regardless of whether the alter is a neighbor or lives farther away. The *proportion* of strong ties that are with neighbors will be higher in general for the foreign-born and for those in low-poverty strata.

Findings

The level of homophily is consistently high for all racial and ethnic groups in Los Angeles County. Table 6.1 presents the level of homophily for the respondent and each alter and then a weighted average of all alters. For each of the three potential alters, the level of homophily is remarkably similar, suggesting that the order of alters has little effect on racial or ethnic homophily and that the alters

Table 6.1   Crosstabulation of level of racial/ethnic homophily for each respondent by alter

R's race / ethnicity	Race/Ethnicity of Alter 1 (N=2,595)					
	Black	Hisp.	Asian	N-H White	Other	Total
Black	**.828**	.032	.002	.135	.003	1
Hispanic	.021	**.820**	.009	.134	.016	1
Asian	.006	.023	**.837**	.106	.029	1
White	.024	.070	.030	**.871**	.006	1

Design-based F (7.70, 3,928.61) = 220.59 p=0.0000

R's race / ethnicity	Race/Ethnicity of Alter 2 (N=2,212)					
	Black	Hisp.	Asian	N-H White	Other	Total
Black	**.828**	.053	.043	.071	.005	1
Hispanic	.039	**.804**	.014	.140	.003	1
Asian	.017	.011	**.911**	.060	.001	1
White	.029	.072	.037	**.848**	.014	1

Design-based F (7.41, 3,653.19) = 175.92 p=0.0000

R's race / ethnicity	Race/Ethnicity of Alter 3 (N=1,763)					
	Black	Hisp.	Asian	N-H White	Other	Total
Black	**.793**	.046	.040	.093	.028	1
Hispanic	.016	**.809**	.016	.150	.009	1
Asian	.016	.060	**.810**	.109	.005	1
White	.037	.089	.028	**.820**	.027	1

Design-based F (9.44, 4,381.31) = 99.33 p=0.0000

Weighted average, with ratio of observed/expected values for homophily based on group population size in Los Angeles County

R's race	BL	O/E	HIS	O/E	AS	O/E	WH	O/E	OTH
BL	**.819**	6.50	.043	.12	.026	.43	.102	.23	.011
HIS	.026	.20	**.812**	2.23	.013	.20	.140	.31	.010
AS	.012	.10	.029	.08	**.855**	14.01	.091	.20	.013
WH	.029	.23	.076	.21	.032	.52	**.850**	1.90	.014

can be averaged with little loss of information. However, having a greater number of alters increases the probability that at least one of them will be heterogeneous.

Even though each racial and ethnic group makes up a widely varying proportion of the population, the level of homophily varies little, only from 81 to 86 percent. As a result, there exists strong variation in the ratio of observed levels of homophily to what would be expected if strong ties were distributed randomly among the population of Los Angeles County. For example, because Hispanics comprise 37 percent of the 1990 population of Los Angeles County, they would be more likely to have strong ties with other Hispanics than with Asians, who comprise less than 11 percent of the population. Their similar levels of homophily show that Hispanics are only twice as likely to associate with one another than they would by chance, whereas Asians are 14 times as likely to associate with other Asians.

Non-Hispanic whites are overwhelmingly the most popular out-group among minorities. This is probably a function of both group size and status. Whites make up 9 percent of Asians' strong ties and 14 percent of Hispanics' ties, but these percentages are far below what would be expected by mere chance. The level of interracial strong ties among minorities is minuscule – no more than 4 percent.

Mathematically, in a small group of generated names (e.g. three confidants), the expected number of interracial or interethnic contacts would be greatest when all contexts have equal portions of minorities (Feld and Carter 1998). Given that, one would expect heterogeneity of strong ties in Los Angeles, where no racial or ethnic group holds a majority. Yet the high proportion of racial and ethnic homophily among co-ethnic ties suggests that racial and ethnic constraints on networks matter more than sheer group size. This high level of racial and ethnic homophily sustains previous findings that the dimension of race is highly salient (Shrum, Cheek, and Hunter 1988).

Table 6.2 Mean proportion of strong ties that are homophilous among those of Mexican and Asian origin, by place of residence and nativity

Group Birthplace	Grand mean (1)	N[b] (2)	Outside concentration — Type of strata — All (3)	Poor (4)	Low-pov (5)	In concentration — Type of strata — All (6)	Poor (7)	Low-pov (8)
Mexican								
U.S.	.693	315	.623	.818	.613	.806	.895	.709
Foreign	.835	849	.814	.834	.807	.851	.871	.765
Asian								
U.S.	.575	211	.498	N/a	.498	.688	.687	.688
Foreign	.939	896	.966	.971	.963	.913	.976	.896

a. Residence in a co-ethnic concentration is defined for Mexicans as living in a stratum in which at least 50 percent of the population is Hispanic. For Asians, the cutoff point for a concentration is 10 percent. Some strata are "mixed," with no predominant group.
b. N refers to the total number of ties with alters, not to the total respondents.

Table 6.2 shows that immigrants have more homophilous strong ties than the native-born of the same racial and ethnic groups. It further shows that these differences interact with residence in a co-ethnic concentration and in wealthier areas. This table shows results from a subsample of those of Mexican and Asian origin, since these are the groups with substantial native and foreign-born populations. Column 1 shows substantial differences between the native-born and foreign-born overall. Among foreign-born Mexicans, 84 percent of their strong ties are with co-ethnics. The level of homophily drops to 70 percent among the native-born, though the difference is not significant. Among those born in Asia, nearly 94 percent of their strong ties are with co-ethnics. But for Asians, the drop in homophily between foreign- and native-born generations is steeper and statistically significant and probably reflects in part the relatively small size of the Asian population. With more than two-fifths of native-born Asians' strong ties crossing racial and ethnic boundaries, the level of homophily shows significant incorporation of this population. These results support the first hypothesis, that immigrants are more homophilous in their strong ties than the native-born.

Columns 3 and 6 display the difference between residence inside and outside a co-ethnic concentration. Among the foreign-born, both Asian and Mexican, residence in a co-ethnic concentration makes no difference in the level of homophily. Those living among other groups are just as likely to forge their strong ties among co-ethnics. These foreign-born may be spatially assimilated, but they are associating heavily with their own racial and ethnic groups regardless of where they live. Among the native-born, however, place of residence makes a difference in the level of homophily in strong ties. Native-born respondents who live outside a co-ethnic concentration are nearly 20 percentage points more likely to have interracial or interethnic strong ties than those inside one. Among native-born Asians in neighborhoods with few fellow Asians, half of their strong ties are with members of other races. This finding supports the second hypothesis, that adult immigrants will maintain homophilous ties regardless of where they live, while neighborhood factors will affect the native-born.

Table 6.3 Mean proportion of ties with neighbors and racial/ethnic homophily for respondents of Mexican origin, by residence in co-ethnic concentration and by nativity

| Mean proportion of homophily | Place of birth | Residence | | | |
| | | Outside concentration[a] | | Inside concentration | |
		Poor[b] strata	Low-pov.	Poor strata	Low-pov.
Tie with neighbor	U.S.	N/a	.615	.923	.806
More distant tie		.763	.616	.868	.564
Tie with neighbor	Foreign	.865	.760	.908	.746
More distant tie		.820	.846	.843	.801
Mean proportion of all strong ties with neighbors	U.S.	.283	.316	.482	.542
	Foreign	.401	.437	.562	.687
Ratio of observed/ expected homophilous ties with neighbors[c]	U.S.	N/a	2.607	.997	1.142
	Foreign	2.285	3.002	1.102	1.414

a. Mexicans living in census tracts that were more than 50 percent Hispanic in 1990 were considered to be in an enclave.
b. In high-poverty strata, more than 40 percent of residents were below the poverty line, according to the 1990 census. In low-poverty strata, less than 20 percent were poor. Medium-poverty strata lay in between.
c. Expected values are based on the percentage of Hispanics in the respondent's block group in the 1990 census.

The effect of wealth on the level of homophily is less clearcut. For Mexicans, the decrease in homophily seems to be confined to wealthier areas, regardless of ethnic concentration. In areas of high or medium poverty, where more than 20 percent of the households fall below the poverty line, the level of homophily remains as high for the native-born as for immigrants, as columns 4 and 7 show. For Asians, the economic status of their neighborhood does not matter for the level of homophily in strong ties, as columns 7 and 8 show. This part of the analysis is confined to co-ethnic areas because the survey picked up few Asians living in poor areas outside a co-ethnic concentration. These mixed findings only partially support the third hypothesis, which had predicted an interaction of wealthier neighborhoods with nativity. For native-born Mexican-Americans, attaining a socioeconomic status that allows them to live in wealthier areas translates into more varied strong ties, but this interaction does not pertain to Asians.

Table 6.4   Logistic regression for ties that are completely homophilous vs. heterogeneous, by ethnic group, nativity, language and neighborhood

	Model 1	Model 2	Model 3	Model 4	Model 5
Mexican origin					
Foreign-born	1.0286**	.8794**	.6224*	.1457	.0211
Co-ethnic concentration		.8693*	.3232		.2457
Neighborhood status			-.8502**		-.7868**
Limited English				1.2575**	.9043*
F	10.77	8.18	8.23	7.48	6.86
Asian origin					
Foreign-born	2.6620***	2.6980***	2.8483***	2.2715**	2.4422***
Co-ethnic concentration		-.2648	-.3121		-.5970
Neighborhood status			.2173		.2322
Limited English				1.2300**	1.4284**
F	17.81	11.56	10.11	13.02	13.96

$p < .05$, ** $p < .01$, *** $p < .001$, two-tailed test

Thus far, it has been impossible to distinguish whether these results are due to the neighborhood factors or to personal characteristics of immigrants. One might argue that immigrants who speak English poorly would be unlikely to discuss *anything* – let alone "important matters" – with someone from a racial or ethnic group that does not share their same native language. Table 6.4 tests the effect of both English-language skills and neighborhood characteristics. The dummy variable for language covers those who report their speaking ability in English as "just fair" or less. For both those of Mexican and Asian origin, those with limited English are significantly more likely than others to have only co-ethnic strong ties, as models 4 and 5 show.

However, the regression also reveals considerable differences between the Mexicans and the Asians. While the foreign-born of both groups are more likely than the native-born to maintain strong ties only with co-ethnics, as Model 1 shows, that difference can be completely explained among Mexicans by language ability and neighborhood context. Among Asians, the distinction between the foreign-born and native-born is much higher than for Mexicans, and it persists at that high level regardless of language ability or neighborhood. Differences beyond language barriers keep foreign-born Asians from forging strong ties with non-Asians. Moreover, for Asians, the effects of neighborhood are slight, and the coefficients run counterintuitively. However, this may be an artifact of the fairly low concentration of Asians even in neighborhoods that are considered Asian concentrations. And as noted before, the Asian data are subject to bias.

Among those of Mexican origin, living in a Hispanic concentration begins to attenuate the effect of foreign birth on ties (Model 2). Living in a poor neighborhood reduces the effect of Mexican birth further (Model 3) and shows that the status of a neighborhood has far more influence than its ethnic concentration. However, poor English alone can explain why those of foreign birth have solely co-ethnic ties rather than ties to other groups (Model 4). In the full model (Model 5), both low-status neighborhoods and limited English influence the level of homophily in strong ties.

The importance of Model 5 rests in what is *not* significant: residence in a co-ethnic concentration. This finding puts the model in slight conflict with the traditional spatial assimilation model, which assumes that attaining residence outside a co-ethnic concentration promotes greater structural incorporation. This model suggests that ethnic composition of the neighborhood does not matter, net of neighborhood status. Why should this be so, since it seems counterintuitive for ethnic composition of the neighborhood to be unrelated to the level of ethnic ties? The most obvious explanation is that people want homophily in their strong ties more than they need to have strong ties with people very close by. This explanation would be in keeping with a long ecological tradition viewing the neighborhood as a "community of limited liability" with restricted social roles or as a place where relationships are strongest for the place-bound and voluntary for everyone else (Greer 1962, Keller 1968, Fischer 1984). The explanation would also be in keeping with network theorists who argue that most social ties lie beyond the immediate neighborhood (Wellman and Wortley 1990). If this preference for homophily over proximity is valid, it should follow that:

1. The level of homophily in strong ties will be roughly the same inside a co-ethnic concentration as outside, since people are seeking out others like themselves.

2. The level of homophily in strong ties will be roughly with same with neighbors as with those more distant.

3. People living outside a co-ethnic concentration will have fewer strong ties with their neighbors than people inside one, because they have fewer co-ethnics with whom they could associate.

4. The observed-to-expected ratio of homophily for those living outside a co-ethnic concentration will be higher than the observed-to-expected ratio for those within one.

Table 6.5 lends support to all of these propositions, at least for the Mexican-origin population (the Asian population contained too few neighborhood ties for disaggregation). The top rows show the mean level of homophily by co-ethnic concentration, neighborhood wealth, nativity, and proximity to the strong tie. Living among co-ethnics appears to matter little, apart from these other characteristics. For instance, among the Mexican-born in low-poverty areas with ties to neighbors, the level of homophily was .746 inside a co-ethnic concentration and .760 outside it. This similarity supports the first proposition. The level of homophily for neighborhood ties was also remarkably similar to that for more distant ties, net of other traits. The only exception was among the native-born living in wealthier co-ethnic concentration, but here the differences are not meaningful because of small sample sizes. This similarity supports the second proposition. Notably, the results for nativity showed little difference between the native-born and the foreign-born.

The middle rows of Table 5 support the third proposition. The proportion of all strong ties that are with neighbors drops substantially depending on whether

| Table 6.5 | Weighted average proportion of ties with neighbors and racial/ethnic homophily for respondents of Mexican origin, by co-ethnic residence and nativity |

Mean proportion of homophily	Place of birth	Residence			
		Outside co-ethnic concentration[a]		Inside co-ethnic concentration	
		High-med poverty[b]	Low-poverty	High-med poverty	Low-poverty
Neighbor tie	U.S.	N/a	.615	.923	.806
More distant tie		.763	.616	.868	.564
Neighbor tie	Foreign	.865	.760	.908	.746
More distant tie		.820	.846	.843	.801
Mean proportion of all strong ties with neighbors	U.S.	.283	.316	.482	.542
	Foreign	.401	.437	.562	.687

Ratio observed/ expected homophilous ties with neighbors[c]

	U.S.	N/a	2.607	.997	1.142
	Foreign	2.285	3.002	1.102	1.414

1. Mexicans living in census tracts that were more than 50 percent Hispanic in 1990 were considered to be in an enclave.
2. In high-poverty strata, more than 40 percent of residents were below the poverty line, according to the 1990 census. In low-poverty strata, less than 20 percent were poor. Medium-poverty strata lay in between.
3. Expected values are based on the percentage of Hispanics in the respondent's block group in the 1990 census.

respondents live in Hispanic enclaves. While foreign birth and neighborhood poverty also appear somewhat influential, Mexicans living within enclaves have significantly greater proportions of strong ties with their neighbors than do those outside enclaves. The differences range from 16 percentage points among the Mexican-born in poor areas to 25 percentage points among the Mexican-born in wealthier areas. The foreign-born in wealthier enclaves have the greatest proportion of their strong ties with neighbors, at nearly 69 percent. The native-born in poorer areas outside Hispanic enclaves have the smallest proportion of their strong ties with neighbors, at 28 percent. The bottom rows support the last proposition, through a ratio created by dividing the mean proportion of homophilous ties with neighbors by an expected value taken from the 1990 census records of the proportion Hispanic of the resident's block group. The ratio is roughly even within Hispanic enclaves, as one might expect. Outside the enclave, however, the ratio rises to at least 2 to 1 and thereby shows a clear preference among those of Mexican origin for neighbors who are co-ethnic. Even though these residents may be considered spatially assimilated, their preference for homophily remains.

Taken together, Table 5 suggests somewhat different types of neighboring patterns depending on whether the respondent lives in a Hispanic enclave. Residents of neighborhoods with a co-ethnic concentration are significantly more likely than those living outside such neighborhoods to report strong ties with neighbors, regardless of nativity or the wealth of the neighborhood. Residents of wealthier areas report more ties with neighbors than those in areas of high or medium poverty. The foreign-born are also consistently more likely to have more of their strong ties within the neighborhood, regardless of where they live. Those living outside Hispanic enclaves seem more likely to have social networks that extend beyond the neighborhood. The overall high level of homophily both inside and outside co-ethnic enclaves suggests that in areas with relatively few Hispanics, residents of Mexican origin still seek out those co-ethnics who *are* there. This is borne out by the higher observed-to-expected ratios outside the enclave. This preference for homophily, even when co-ethnics are relatively few in number, undermines the old Chicago School idea that spatial distance is a useful proxy for social distance.

Discussion

By confirming the expectation that immigrants have substantially greater racial and ethnic homophily in their strong ties than the native-born, this chapter offers a new way of examining immigrants' integration. Strong ties represent confidants – not just contacts – and the kind of social support that Gordon (1964) labeled structural assimilation. If successive immigrant generations show a drop in the level of homophily with other racial and ethnic groups, it is a sign of integration. This measurement of homophilous ties has the advantage of being more direct than the customary measurement of spatial assimilation, which considers only where immigrants reside and must assume that relationships develop among racially and ethnically dissimilar people who live near one another. In fact, this assumption inherent in spatial assimilation is only partially borne out here. As Table 6.4 shows, the change in the level of homophily in ties with neighbors is slight between those of Mexican origin who live in a co-ethnic concentration and those who do not. Instead, residence outside a co-ethnic concentration is associated with fewer strong ties with neighbors. However, this pattern of homophily holds most strongly for the immigrant generation. Among the native-born – and particularly among the native-born in wealthier strata – the level of homophily among neighborhood ties drops, in keeping with the spatial assimilation perspective. Still, despite these lower levels of homophily, more than 60 percent of the strong ties of spatially assimilated, U.S-born citizens of Mexican origin are with fellow Hispanics.

Another major finding concerns the significant variation in overall levels of racial and ethnic homophily between those who live among co-ethnics and those who do not. This was my second hypothesis, and it was strongly supported. Residents of co-ethnic concentrations are much more likely to form strong ties with other co-ethnics. Moreover, the expected interaction of immigrant status and residence appears. Immigrants and the native-born show relatively little difference in the level of racial and ethnic homophily in their strong ties when they are residents of enclaves. However, among those who do not live among co-ethnics, immigrants are more likely than the native-born to maintain co-ethnic strong ties. These findings support the idea of "heterolocal" ties advanced by Zelinsky and Lee (1998).

The status of the neighborhood also affects the level of homophily in strong ties, as the third hypothesis predicted. Those of Mexican and Asian origin in high-poverty areas have high levels of homophily. Those in low-poverty areas show much more variability, depending on nativity. The native-born have much lower levels of homophily than the foreign-born. This interaction shows that intergroup strong ties are most likely among those living outside ethnic enclaves in wealthier areas. The level of intergroup ties is negligible elsewhere. It is impossible to make a truly causal argument here, since the cross-sectional data do not show whether residence outside an enclave preceded intergroup ties. But since neighborhood is generally considered a contextual variable and is less mutable than friendship patterns, it seems reasonable to argue that neighborhood status influences the composition of strong ties rather than the other way around. Certainly, such an argument is in line with traditional arguments for spatial assimilation.

But the traditional argument for spatial assimilation assumes that the first generation is unlikely to leave poor ethnic enclaves for decades, if at all. For that reason, spatial assimilation theory never clearly distinguishes whether moving to the suburbs was a sign of socioeconomic mobility or social integration. However, in the last 30 years, ethnic concentrations have sprung up in suburbs, and some well-to-do immigrants have settled directly in neighborhoods populated largely by the native-born white middle-class (Zelinsky and Lee 1998). The findings here provide empirical evidence to support Zelinsky and Lee's contention that immigrants maintain co-ethnic ties even when such ties may not be in the same neighborhood.

At least among Mexican immigrants, the first-generation is more likely than the native-born to have strong ties with neighbors, as the fourth hypothesis predicted. This pattern persists even outside Hispanic enclaves, where more than 40 percent of Mexican immigrants' reported strong ties are with neighbors. These ties are highly homophilous and may reflect the uniquely large size of the Mexican immigrant population. Many non-Mexican neighborhoods still have sizable Mexican minorities (Allen and Turner 1997), so that Mexican immigrants outside an actual enclave still have easy access to many co-ethnics. Among Asians, a much smaller proportion of both immigrants and native-born report any strong ties with neighbors. Even so, the Mexican immigrants' proclivity to have many of their ties with neighbors must temper any tendency to define immigrants' social ties as liberated from spatial constraints.

CHAPTER 7
Conclusion: The Community Typology and Immigrants

What has emerged from the last three chapters is an explanation of the extent to which immigrants have strong ties, what kinds of ties they have and with whom they hold them. Bound up in this explanation is the importance of place of residence, particularly whether immigrants live among co-ethnics, and how residence as well as individual attributes influence the size and composition of networks. Do these data tell a coherent story? They seem to. While the results are not generalizable beyond Los Angeles County, the patterns are likely to appear in other cities as well.

Immigrants tend to have fewer strong ties outside the household than the native-born. That was clear from Chapter 3. Among those immigrants who *do* have strong ties, those ties are more likely to be with non-kin (though in this regard, immigrants are like internal migrants). The ties also are more often with neighbors than with alters living farther away. That finding, though not strong, emerged from Chapter 5. Immigrants' strong ties are also more likely to be homophilous racially and ethnically. This came out of Chapter 6. Thus, the strong ties of immigrants are

111

fewer, more localized (especially for Hispanics in Los Angeles), and more similar to one another than the strong ties of U.S. natives.

This pattern suggests that immigrants have fewer options than the native-born in whom they can turn to for emotional and social support. Small group size usually portends integration, but not necessarily when immigrants are so distinctive along so many salient parameters. In their case, distinctiveness fosters in-group cohesion. At the same time, their smaller group size constrains their options for forming strong ties. By the very fact that immigrants left a homeland, they also probably left behind kinship ties on which they might have been able to draw. Indeed, as the means from the appendix show, migrants overall have fewer kinship ties than natives, although the results are not clear-cut. As a result, migrants are more dependent on non-kin – friends, co-workers and neighbors – for their supportive relationships. These non-kin relationships need more nurturing than kinship ties. Further, the propinquity and homophily of immigrants' strong relationships suggest that immigrants are less likely than natives to have many of the sorts of weaker relationships that could serve as an entrée to jobs or other opportunities.

Compounding the difficulty of immigrants in forming and sustaining strong ties is the firm link, shown in Chapter 3, between socioeconomic status and social ties. Poverty and low education are strongly associated with fewer strong ties outside the household. Because human capital can be turned into social capital, making and keeping non-kin ties is particularly hard for people with little human capital. They lack the savoir-faire, the money and possibly even the access to transportation necessary to engage in the reciprocal exchanges that sustain such relationships. The jobless may lack the motivation to leave their neighborhoods regularly. This may explain part of the association between low socioeconomic status and strong ties within the neighborhood. Immigrants are particularly disadvantaged, not only because many of them are relatively unskilled and unschooled, but because they also have distinctive language and customs that restrict their choices to fellow expatriates.

Yet this set of findings about the difficulty of immigrants in developing and sustaining strong ties runs utterly contrary to migration theory. Prevailing theory holds that migrants "draw upon obligations implicit in relationships such as kinship and friendship to gain access to employment and assistance at the point of destination" (Massey et al. 1998: 43). This is a strongly networked approach to immigrant social relations. It tends to see each act of migration as contributing to the social capital of the entire community, or at least an immigrant's entire network of acquaintances. Later migrants can draw on that social capital.

But the nature of strong ties as one form of social capital is that such ties are micro-level. They thrive on reciprocity. These ties are fueled by personal interaction. Kinship ties may endure longer separations and greater inequality in contributions, but other types of strong ties change with the life cycle. The implicit obligations to which migration theorists refer are not necessarily permanent or adaptable to every member of a community.

As the results of this study show, individuals who lack resources – be they money or education or even health – are less likely to be able to take advantage of the collective nature of social capital. These findings complement previous ethnographic research (Mahler 1995, Menjívar 2000) showing how poverty restricts the ability of

Salvadoran immigrants to lend aid to one another. The findings also dovetail with those of Roschelle (1997), who found the greatest extended support networks among the middle-class and non-Hispanic whites. Poverty weakens the bonds of immigrant networks. To outsiders, such as employers, networks of first-generation immigrants may look tight and supportive, because the immigrants that the outsiders meet are those in such networks. But the results here suggest that a substantial proportion of immigrants may not be part of such networks and thus never show up in snowball samples.

The greatest gap in the presence of strong ties appears in the first generation. Among native Hispanics and Asians, the proportion reporting strong ties outside the household rises, as does the diversity of those ties in terms of neighborhood and race/ethnicity. The greater breadth and depth of strong ties suggest that the native-born members of these groups are forging broad, integrative ties beyond the ethnic enclave. While one cannot conclude that micro-level findings of integration signal macro-level evidence of assimilation, the results at least are suggestive. However, findings for blacks and whites are less clear, both because of sample size and inability to determine specific ethnic background for white alters. Also, one must bear in mind the possibility of cultural bias, if first-generation immigrants interpret the concept of "important discussants" differently from natives. One study considers the potential bias minimal (Blau et al. 1991); nevertheless, further research on this question is warranted.

Residence among co-ethnics plays an important role in structuring choices of strong ties, though the causal direction is unclear. People with strong in-group preferences may choose to live among co-ethnics, or living among co-ethnics may constrain the available sets of potential non-kin ties. Either way, people who live among co-ethnics are more likely to have co-ethnic ties than those who live outside co-ethnic areas. Within co-ethnic areas, the native- and foreign-born have roughly the same proportion of strong ties among co-ethnics. Outside co-ethnic areas, however, the native-born have more diverse ties, while the foreign-born maintain somewhat more homophilous ties. This finding also indicates greater racial and ethnic integration among the native-born, though only among those who live *outside* co-ethnic concentrations.

Such findings bolster Massey's (1985) argument that spatial assimilation is a necessary precondition to structural assimilation. This is important, because the study of spatial assimilation has long hinged on the assumption that residence in neighborhoods of out-groups (presumably, ethnic and racial minorities settling among non-Hispanic whites) would foster greater interracial contact. This study provides micro-level confirmation that such interaction occurs, at least for second or later generations.

As for the actual number of ties, non-Hispanic whites tend to have many more strong ties overall when they live among co-ethnics and non-whites more strong ties when they are *outside* ethnic concentrations, as the weighted means from Chapter 3 show. But this difference tends to be explained by the socioeconomic characteristics of the individual; these individual traits attenuate the racial and socioeconomic status characteristics of the neighborhood. Nothing about these results suggests that a minority neighborhood itself hinders the formation of strong ties. At least at the level of strong ties, these findings do not support an ecological explanation, such as Wilson's (1987), that the concentrated poverty of the ghetto accentuates the isolation of the underclass. Rather, these findings extend to immigrants the argument by Fernandez and Harris (1992) that social isolation takes place at the individual level. Of course, it would be useful to try to duplicate these results with a data set that lent itself to a random-effects model at the contextual level.

The next question is how to relate these findings to the network-analytic typology of community devised by Wellman (1979). The importance of individual characteristics as opposed to neighborhood characteristics in determining the overall number of strong ties suggests the importance of the embeddedness of the *individual* within a social structure. Of course, neighborhood is part of that social structure, but people tend to have some choice about where they live (although especially among the poor, that choice may be heavily constrained). Given the limited nature of the cross-sectional data used here, drawing strong theoretical conclusions would be foolhardy. Nonetheless, the data appear to sustain a network-based approach to the idea of community as opposed to a purely ecological one. Even an urban village – the classic "community saved" – seems to consist of a series of closely linked networks of people who chose or perhaps felt they had no choice but to maintain ties close to home. Place then becomes one dimension of the social structure.

Yet place remains crucial in any conception of networks. As Wellman has acknowledged (1996), even the "community liberated" is not truly liberated from space. Most social relationships are with people who live less than an hour away, if not in the immediate neighborhood. The "community without propinquity" can sustain weak ties but not strong ones, which require face-to-face interaction or they will wither. Just such attenuation may occur in the long separations required by immigration. Homans' dictum about interaction and sentiment means that strong ties *require* some propinquity.

So if the community types delineated by Wellman contain both network and spatial aspects, it becomes possible to synthesize Wellman's communities into one micro-level framework, as in Table 7.1. These four types are mutually exclusive. Those people in the "community saved" are those whose strong ties are only within their immediate neighborhood. Those in the "community liberated" have their strong ties outside the neighborhood. Those in the "community mediate" have ties both in the neighborhood and beyond it. Those in the "community lost" have no strong ties, only weak ones. This conceptualization smoothes out the theoretical differences between the old models of "lost," "saved," and "liberated," so that they are no longer competing paradigms for the organization of community. Rather, this conceptualization views community not, on the one hand, as ecologically determined or, on the other hand, as aspatial, but as a web of place-linked networks in which individuals are embedded.

Table 7.1	Framework for applying the community typologies			
	Community Type			
	Saved	Mediate	Liberated	Lost
Strength of tie	Strong and weak	Strong and weak	Strong and weak	Weak only
Strong tie location	Neighborhood-based	Neighborhood-based and beyond	Beyond the neighborhood	N/A

Because these cells are mutually exclusive, it is possible to quantify the proportion of the population in each column. This is mainly a heuristic devise, since the

Beyond the Immigrant Enclave

proportion of the community mediate is likely to grow as the number of alters sought increases. But even if the proportion of ties in each category depends on the number of alters, the *differences* in proportion across racial and ethnic groups should remain a useful indicator. As Table 7.2 shows, even in as small a network as three alters, some telling patterns begin to emerge. Results are shown for non-Hispanic whites and Mexicans, because each has a large sample of foreign-born and native-born, as well as for all non-Hispanic blacks and native-born blacks. The existence of a community "saved" for all three groups is noteworthy, in that a substantial proportion of the population still draws on neighborhood ties exclusively. This community "saved" is smallest for blacks, and largest for Mexicans, particularly the foreign-born. Blacks in Los Angeles County tend more toward ties outside the neighborhood than either whites or Mexicans. Nativity appears to affect the location of social networks of those of Mexican origin. Among the foreign-born, local ties appear much more commonplace than among the native-born.

Table 7.2	Distribution of community types among Angelenos, by race/ethnicity and nativity				
	Community Type				Ratio of saved to liberated
	Saved	Mediate	Liberated	Lost	
N-H white	.177	.320	.392	.111	.452
Foreign-born	.181	.348	.326	.145	.555
Native-born	.176	.314	.405	.104	.435
N-H black	.117	.237	.412	.234	.284
Native-born	.112	.260	.376	.252	.298
Mexican	.199	.192	.227	.382	.877
Foreign-born	.217	.176	.178	.428	1.219
Native-born	.160	.223	.326	.291	.491

This variation shows up well in the ratio of the proportion of respondents in a community saved to the proportion liberated. The higher the number, the greater the group's tendency toward neighborhood rather than distal ties. Only for the Mexican-born is the ratio higher than parity. Native-born Mexicans are more than twice as likely to have distal ties than neighborhood ones. This ratio approaches that of non-Hispanic whites, suggesting that at least in the spatial configuration of social networks, Mexicans are adapting a mainstream pattern.

The likelihood of respondents holding different types of community ties also depends on the characteristics of the neighborhood. In Los Angeles, more than 35 percent of those sampled live outside a co-ethnic concentration. What makes that 35 percent different from those inside a co-ethnic concentration is the racial and ethnic diversity in their strong ties. As Chapter 6 shows, these residents have much lower levels of homophily, particularly in the relatively unusual situation when their only strong ties are with neighbors. The nature of their strong ties is substantively different, and that difference is associated with, if not caused by, place of residence.

For this reason, a network analysis of urban social ties needs to consider the effect of place – neighborhood ethnic composition being only one element of that – as part of the social structure in which ties are embedded. The "community liberated" perspective may have developed as a way of showing how personal networks need not be bound to neighborhood, but that in no way precludes neighborhoods from structuring networks. Empirically, several networks studies have shown the relationship between neighborhood and networks (e.g. Oliver 1988, Mouw and Entwistle 2001, Faust et al. 1999). But theoretically, little work has synthesized place and networks (but see Lee and Campbell 1999). Much of the empirical work centers on responses to Wilson (1987) about how social isolation in the ghetto affects job-hunting (e.g. Johnson et al. 2000). The relatively little empirical and theoretical work relating immigration to social networks and space focuses largely on how the second generation, often growing up in poor neighborhoods, tends to perform either extremely well or badly (e.g. Zhou and Bankston 1998). But beyond labor research and the model of "segmented assimilation," immigration studies of networks have tended to look at transnational migrant flows rather than adaptation at the point of destination.

As a result, the study of how networks and place shape immigrant adaptation is ripe for more work. This study has shown that place residence is strongly associated with the composition of the alters whom individuals cultivate as strong ties. It has also shown substantial effects between the first and later generations, mediated by place. Last, it has attempted to synthesize disparate ecological and network-based conceptions of community into a coherent framework.

More broadly, the transnational migration work has seemed to assume that the kin and friendship networks that encouraged immigration in the first place sustain the immigrants over the long run. The studies by Mahler, Roschelle and Menjívar have questioned this assumption. Further empirical work would be justified, from both a social and policy standpoint, to ascertain the degree to which immigrants can genuinely rely on their sponsors. Portes' work on the importance of the context of reception would suggest that those groups who have faced the most discrimination and governmental neglect would have relatively fragile networks, as Mahler's and Menjívar's studies of illegal Salvadorans illustrate.

Moreover, domestic immigrant networks have not tended to be studied for range, multiplexity, centrality and other characteristics that might illustrate differences between immigrants' and natives' networks. The varying levels of homophily found in Chapter 6 of this study suggest that immigrants may well have different types of networks from the native-born. Such differences would affect immigrants' opportunities and social support, particularly if more studies substantiated the finding of substantially fewer strong ties among immigrants.

Another focus for further work is the dimension of residence. As numerous studies have shown, ethnic enclaves are not necessarily cohesive bastions or a *Klasse für sich*. Nor are immigrants who settle in suburbs dominated by the native-born necessarily welcomed into broader native social circles. The interaction between immigrants and their neighbors (or the lack of it) would help to illuminate the idea of context of reception and to show how immigrants adapt and how the process of assimilation begins at a micro level. The evidence from this study shows that a lack of resources – money, education and employment – is strongly associated with fewer strong ties outside the household. In that case, many enclaves may be much lonelier places than often assumed.

In terms of policy, social isolation among immigrants could have great effects for disseminating job information and training and many kinds of social support. When people need help, they are less likely to get it from friends and relatives if they have fewer friends and relatives on whom to draw. As Chapter 5 showed, migrants in general (and by definition, all immigrants are migrants) tend to have fewer strong kinship ties than the natives of a city. Yet immigrants are the least likely to have the time and resources for making and keeping friends. They rely more on neighbors, and such relationships tend to end once one party moves. All of these factors limit the amount of social support available to immigrants and probably mean that getting information out to immigrants is particularly difficult. Opportunities to increase human capital, and in particular job training and English classes, would enhance the ability of immigrants to forge new relationships.

APPENDIX A
The Survey Instrument

With 4,025 respondents, the Los Angeles segment of the Multi-City Study of Urban Inequality (MCSUI) is by far the largest. Moreover, it offers a greater variable of ethnic groups, many of whom are immigrants, than the other cities in the survey. The only exception is Boston, where the sample includes several hundred Puerto Ricans and Dominicans. In Los Angeles, the Hispanics tend to be Puerto Rican or Dominican in Boston and Mexican, Mexican-American or Salvadoran. The Asians, sampled extensively only in Los Angeles, comprise mostly Koreans and Chinese, with some Japanese.[4]

The MCSUI consists of a multi-stage, clustered probability survey that oversampled census tracts with concentrations of the poor and minorities. Between 1992 and 1993, face-to-face interviews were conducted in each city with randomly selected adults of at least 21 years of age in the sampled households. Interviewers went to the respondents' homes. To minimize any cultural bias,

---

[4] The study did not consider Filipinos.

The MCSUI does not break out Asians by ethnicity. My thanks to David M. Grant for providing data from the original Los Angeles Study of Urban Inequality so that I could examine specific groups.

investigators relied on co-ethnic interviewers wherever possible.

These individual-level data are geolinked to selected variables from the STF3 file of the 1990 U.S. Census of Population and Housing at the block-group level, but data identifying the particular block group have been removed. By providing random samples by type of neighborhood, this survey picks up social isolates and avoids the selectivity bias inherent in data-gathering approaches that collect network information only on those persons with certain kinds of ties (Marsden and Hurlbert 1987).

The LA framework is based on all the census tracts in Los Angeles County, which comprises 4,083 square miles and had a 1990 population of 8.9 million. Investigators created the sampling frame by allocating more than 1,600 census tracts to seven strata according to race and ethnicity. For Japanese, Chinese, and Koreans, the threshold for an ethnic stratum consisted of 10 percent of the population; for blacks, non-Hispanic whites and Hispanics, the threshold was 50 percent. These seven strata were then subdivided by poverty level, for a final total of 16 strata. Low-poverty strata were defined as having less than 20 percent of the residents below the poverty line. In high-poverty strata, more than 40 percent were poor; medium-poverty strata lay in between. Because so few Asians and non-Hispanic whites lived in tracts with high poverty, for these groups high- and medium-poverty classifications were collapsed. From these 16 strata, investigators settled on 98 census tracts for the survey. From these, the investigators randomly chose 567 blocks and randomly picked households from the blocks (Bobo et al. 1998).

To account for the sampling frame, the statistical analyses here rely on Stata's survey-design module, which controls for design effects in multistage surveys. It gives accurate parameters, but involves several trade-offs. For one, it uses a pseudo-maximum likelihood estimator, which does not produce a log likelihood. For another, it requires an assumption of fixed neighborhood effects. But the small size of the neighborhood-level clusters (15 percent of all cases are in clusters of three or fewer) militates against a multi-level analysis. I use person-level weights to correct for strata-specific weights and for differences in household size (Bobo et al. 1998, StataCorp. 2001). For most variables, this is appropriate, although household-level weights would be better for income measures.

The Validity of Name Generators

The dependent variable in this analysis consists of a question meant to elicit the respondent's core social network by asking for discussion partners. The actual MCSUI question reads:

> "From time to time, most people discuss important matters with other people. Looking back over the last six months – who are the people, other than people living in your household, with whom you discussed matters important to you? Please tell me the first name or initials of the people with whom you discussed matters important to you. IF LESS THAN 3, PROBE: Anyone else?"

This is a variation on the important-discussant question first used in a special module of the General Social Survey (GSS) in 1985. That question also asked respondents to name all people with whom they had discussed important matters within the last six months. In the GSS, follow-up questions were restricted to the first five names, while the MCSUI uses the first three names. This is a severe restriction, since nearly 40 percent of the GSS sample named four or more alters, though the modal number was three alters (Marsden 1987). Notably, the GSS name-generator question allowed respondents to name a person within their own household, whereas the MCSUI did not.

These two differences may have contradictory effects. On the one hand, limiting the follow-up questions to three instead of five constricts the size of the networks and magnifies the effect of being named first as an alter. Because the first alter cited in the GSS was slightly more likely to be kin – or a spouse – than other alters and because the data report a large number of small networks (Marsden 1987), the MCSUI may be emphasizing kin ties at the expense of friendships. MCSUI may also be emphasizing same-sex ties, since the discussion partners of the same sex tended to be named earlier (Burt 1986). On the other hand, by not allowing respondents to name ties within their own household, the MCSUI is eliminating an obvious source of kin ties. The important point is that these differences make it impossible to compare the level of kinship ties across the two surveys.

The wording of the "important-discussant" question also can be criticized as vague and hard for the respondent to interpret, particularly in a cross-cultural context. Yet the ambiguity of the question was what attracted researchers to it in the first place, because it "identifies comparatively intense portions of the interpersonal environment for all respondents, and it thus has some general utility" (Marsden 1987: 123). The question as originally written by Ronald S. Burt referred not just to important matters but to important *personal* matters. However, the question was broadened to the current wording when pretesting showed that some respondents construed "personal" matters rather narrowly and intimately (Ruan 1998).

Despite the vagueness of the "important-discussant" question, three recent studies tend to confirm its validity. Comparisons between the United States and China find that in both cultures, the "important-discussant" question taps similar particularistic responses (Blau et al. 1991). In another study, respondents asked to interpret "important matters" gave a variety of responses, some of which varied according to the context of the interview (Bailey and Marsden 1999). However, the results found minimal variation between the respondent's interpretation of the question and network composition. As a result, Bailey and Marsden conclude that the "important-matters" question succeeds at eliciting a core discussion network, even if the content of the discussions remains generally unspecified. A third study comparing the "important-matters" question to other types of name-generator questions found that major differences in wording had very minor effect on reports of egocentric networks (Straits 2000).

Analysis of the "important-discussant" question in the GSS has shed light on many questions about egocentric networks. Looking at network structure, Marsden (1987, 1988) showed that many networks were small, dense, based on kinship and homophilous. Huang and Tausig (1990) linked network range and socioeconomic status. Moore (1990) found that women's greater focus on family networks and men's focus on co-workers stemmed largely from structural constraints. Liao and Stevens (1994) investigated the circumstances under which respondents named a spouse as an alter, while Hurlbert and Acock (1990) examine how network structure varies by marital status. Acock and Hurlbert (1993) link marital status to well-being and networks, and Burt (1987) examines the relationship between network density and happiness.

Looking at the workplace, Hurlbert (1991) found that ties among co-workers increased job satisfaction, particularly when co-workers had high levels of education.

Straits (1996) found that men were more likely to report same-sex ties with co-workers and attributed this to social structural variation in the workplace as well as individual choice.

Rural-urban differences were examined by Beggs, Haines and Hurlbert (1996) and Deng and Bonacich (1991). The former find that rural networks are smaller and based more kinship and neighborhood. The latter contradict the idea that urbanism promotes a subculture among blacks.

In studies of politics, Bienenstock et al. (1990) find that network homogeneity and density intensify social and political differences among ethnic and religious groups with identifiable beliefs. Knoke (1990) and Straits (1991) examined political discussion among network members.

Several other surveys have used instruments similar to the GSS to study networks. In Louisiana, Beggs, Hurlbert and Haines (1996) look at community attachment in rural areas. Blau et al. (1991) compare the GSS results to those in a similar survey in Tianjin, China.

Several published studies have also used the network data from the MCSUI. For example, Freeman (2001) uses the network data from all three cities in which they were collected (Atlanta, Boston and Los Angeles) to examine the connection between neighborhood social ties and residential density. Johnson et al. (2000) used the Los Angeles data to examine women's labor-force participation. Research involving the Atlanta data show black-white differences in support networks (Green, Hammer and Tigges 2000). Elliott (1999) examines the relationship between neighborhood and social networks in the job market.

Following previous work (Marsden 1987, Straits 1991, Louch 2000), I am using the "important-discussant" question as a proxy for strong ties. This is not a perfect proxy, for several reasons. First, the exchange of confidences is only part of the definition of a strong tie (Granovetter 1973). These ties often have instrumental components as well, which are not necessarily captured by a question on important discussants. Second, the measurement of strong ties has long been hampered by poor operationalization in which the concept was equated with various indicators. Closeness of the relationship seems to be the most adequate way of capturing the idea (Marsden and Campbell 1984), but even this is vague. Third, many people do not discuss intimate matters even with close friends. Many of their friendships may actually fall into what Wireman (1984) calls "intimate secondary relationships," in which people may be friendly within a given context (e.g. a soccer club or church) but never develop an external relationship. A study among white urban men finds that friendships tend "to be rather circumscribed affairs in which there are relatively restricted exchanges of intimate content" (Laumann 1973: 125). Because of these limitations, my measurement may be omitting some strong ties and thus be conservative.

Independent Variables

This appendix offers further explanation on crucial independent variables and their measurement. Independent variables consist, first, of two neighborhood-level variables. The first is whether the respondent lives in a co-ethnic concentration. Since there exists no classification for identifying the proportion of any ethnic group that must live in a cluster before the area becomes known as a concentration (or, in some cases, an enclave), the demarcation of a co-ethnic concentration is not obvious. To define enclave, Alba, Logan and Crowder (1997) use a standard for overrepresentation in a census tract of two times the proportion of the regional population. But with a large minority, that could become a prohibitive criterion, since the ethnic concentration is also a function of size of the overall population as well as its level of segregation. However, the multi-stage design of the survey offers an ad hoc solution, albeit an imperfect one, to the question of the co-ethnic concentration. Because investigators divided each city into racial and ethnic strata based on census-tract population, the stratum itself can indicate concentration. In the MCSUI, a concentration was taken to be an area that was majority black, non-Hispanic white, or Hispanic. For Asians, the cutoff for concentration was 10 percent of the population.

The second neighborhood-level variable consists of a factor score for neighborhood status, based on characteristics of the resident's census block group. The score derives from the proportion of resident adults with college education, the proportion of owner-occupied housing and the median income. White and Sassler (2000) construct a similar type of variable using principle components analysis of tract-level data on five characteristics. For them, a single component explained 36 percent of the variance; my component explained more than twice that level.

Individual-level variables fall into three groups: demographic, human capital and social capital. Besides race and ethnicity, the demographic ones comprise gender, number of adults in the household, presence of children under age 18, nativity and length of time in the city. The sample has a fairly even distribution of many of these variables.

Among these demographic variables, the presence of other adults in the household would present an alternative source of potential strong ties. Spouses rank consistently as the strongest social tie (Burt 1986). In some analyses, I do not control for spouse per se, because the literature argues that networks tend to affect conjugal relations rather than the other way around (Bott 1955, Milardo and Allan 2000). The presence of children could increase strong ties if parents get to know one another through school activities or play groups. Mothers of young children are often more dependent on the neighborhood, but men living in neighborhoods with many children are also more engaged with neighbors (Bell and Boat 1957, Bridge 1995). However, research on the socializing effect of children suggests that it generally extends only to whites (Sampson et al. 1999). Research among blacks suggests that rearing

children successfully may require more of their parents'
attention and even attempts to isolate their children
(Anderson 1991, Korbin and Coulton 1997). The
neighborhood-effects literature in general is mixed on
whether or how the neighborhood influences children
above and beyond their own families (Brooks-Gunn,
Duncan and Aber, 1997). Traditionally, too, child-bearing
is associated with mobility as parents often buy houses or
search for single-family quarters and neighborhoods with
other children and good schools (Rossi 1980). For
immigrant groups, attaining these amenities generally
requires moving away from co-ethnics. Also, I measure
place of birth, since immigrants would probably have fewer
kin available as potential ties. As for the time variable, I
measure number of years in the city for ties overall and
number of years at the present address for ties with
neighbors.

Characteristics relating to human and social capital are
education, language ability, and income. Education and
English ability are highly correlated, with poor English
found almost exclusively among those with little education.
Education and language ability represent opportunity for or
constraints on greater levels of contact. Low income also
limits the exchange reciprocity necessary to sustain strong
ties.

To account for missing data on family income, I
imputed a weighted mean for the entire sample; that mean
equaled $34,109 in Boston and $44,790 in LA. I then
applied this mean to 340 missing cases in Boston and 680
missing cases in Los Angeles. I also included a dummy
variable for the imputed cases. The initial income question
was topcoded, but those whose income exceeded $150,000
annually were then asked to state their income. For missing

data on this follow-up question, I imputed the median value
for all high-income respondents (this was $185,000 in Los
Angeles).

A caveat is necessary on the measurement of race and
ethnicity. The stratification of the survey imposes arbitrary
restrictions on racial identities. In Los Angeles, for
instance, all respondents are coded as non-Hispanic white,
non-Hispanic black, Hispanic or Asian, regardless of
mixed-race backgrounds. The result makes statistical
analysis easier but disregards the distinction between race
and ethnicity. One can be ethnically Hispanic as well as
white or black or Asian, but not in these data.

References

Abelmann, Nancy and John Lie. 1995. *Blue Dreams: Korean Americans and the Los Angeles Riots*. Cambridge, Mass.: Harvard University Press.

Acock, Alan C. and Jeanne S. Hurlbert. 1993. "Social networks, marital status, and well-being." *Social Networks* 15: 309-334.

Adams, Bert N.. 1967. "Interaction Theory and the Social Network." *Sociometry* 30: 64-78.

Ahlbrandt, Roger S. Jr.. 1984. *Neighborhoods, People and Community*. New York: Plenum Press.

Alba, Richard D. and John R. Logan. 1993. "Minority Proximity to Whites in Suburbs: An Individual-Level Analysis of Segregation." *American Journal of Sociology* 98: 1388-1427.

Alba, Richard D., John R. Logan, and Kyle Crowder. 1997. "White Neighborhoods and Assimilation: The Greater New York Region, 1980-1990." *Social Forces* 75: 883-909.

Alba, Richard D., John R. Logan, Brian J. Stults, Gilbert Marzan, and Wenquan Zhang. 1999. "Immigrant Groups in the Suburbs: A Reexamination of Suburbanization and Spatial Assimilation." *American Sociological Review* 64: 446-460.

137

Alba, Richard, D. and Victor Nee. 1997. "Rethinking Assimilation Theory for a New Era of Immigration." *International Migration Review* 31: 826-874.

------. 2003. *Remaking the American Mainstream: Assimilation and the New Immigration*. Cambridge, Mass.: Harvard University Press.

Allen, James P. and Eugene Turner. 1997. *The Ethnic Quilt: Population Diversity in Southern California*. Northridge, Calif.: The Center for Geographical Studies, California State University, Northridge.

Anderson, Elijah. 1991. "Neighborhood Effects on Teenage Pregnancy." In *The Urban Underclass*, edited by Christopher Jencks and Paul E. Peterson. Washington, D.C.: The Brookings Institution.

Antonucci, Toni C. and Kees C.P.M. Knipscheer. 1990. "Social Network Research: Review and Perspectives," in *Social Network Research: Substantive Issues and Methodological Questions*, edited by C.P.M. Knipscheer and T.C. Antonucci. Amsterdam: Swets & Zeitlinger B.V.

Apollinaire, Guillaume. 1970. *Apollinaire: Alcools*. Edited by R.C.D. Perman. Oxford, England: Basil Blackwell.

Axelrod, Morris. 1956. "Urban Structure and Social Participation." *American Sociological Review* 21: 13-18.

Bailey, Stefanie and Peter V. Marsden. 1999. "Interpretation and interview context: examining the General Social Survey name generator using cognitive methods." *Social Networks* 21: 287-309.

Bailey, Thomas and Roger Waldinger. 1991. "Primary, Secondary, and Enclave Labor Markets: A Training Systems Approach." *American Sociological Review* 56: 432-445.

Bean, Frank D. and Stephanie Bell-Rose. 1999. *Immigration and Opportunity: Race, Ethnicity, and Employment in the United States.* New York: Russell Sage Foundation.

Bean, Frank D., Gillian Stevens, and Susan Wierzbicki. 2003. "The New Immigrants and Theories of Incorporation," In *America's Newcomers: Immigrant Incorporation and the Dynamics of Diversity*, by Frank D. Bean and Gillian Stevens. New York: Russell Sage Foundation.

Beggs, John J., Valerie A. Haines, and Jeanne S. Hurlbert. 1996a. "Revisiting the Rural-Urban Contrast: Personal Networks in Nonmetropolitan and Metropolitan Settings." *Rural Sociology* 61: 306-325.

Beggs, John J., Jeanne S. Hurlbert, and Valerie A. Haines. 1996b. "Community Attachment in a Rural Setting: A Refinement and Empirical Test of the Systemic Model." *Rural Sociology* 61: 407-426.

Bell, Wendell. and Marion D. Boat. 1957. "Urban Neighborhoods and Informal Social Relations." *American Journal of Sociology* 62: 391-398.

Bienenstock, Elisa Jayne, Phillip Bonacich, and Melvin Oliver. 1990. "The Effect of Network Density and Homogeneity on Attitude Polarization." *Social Networks* 12: 153-172.

Blackwell, James E. and Philip S. Hart. 1982. *Cities, Suburbs and Blacks: A Study of Concerns, Distrust and Alienation.* Bayside, N.Y.: General Hall, Inc.

Blau, Peter M. 1977. *Inequality and Heterogeneity.* New York: The Free Press.

Blau, Peter M., Danching Ruan, and Monika Ardelt. 1991. "Interpersonal Choice and Networks in China." *Social Forces* 69: 1037-1062.

Blum, Terry C. 1985. "Structural Constraints on Interpersonal
    Relations: A Test of Blau's Macrosociological Theory."
    American Journal of Sociology 91: 511-521.

Bobo, Lawrence, James Johnson, Melvin Oliver, Reynolds
    Farley, Barry Bluestone, Irene Browne, Sheldon
    Danziger, Gary Green, Harry Holzer, Maria Krysan,
    Michael Massagli, and Camille Zubrinsky Charles.
    1998. *Multi-City Study of Urban Inequality, 1992-1994:
    Atlanta, Boston, Detroit, and Los Angeles.* 2nd ICPSR
    version. Atlanta, GA: Mathematica/ Boston, MA:
    University of Massachusetts, Survey Research
    Laboratory/ Ann Arbor, MI: University of Michigan,
    Detroit Area Study and Institute for Social Research,
    Survey Research Center / Los Angeles, CA: University
    of California, Survey Research Program.

Bodnar, John. 1985. *The Transplanted: A History of Immigrants
    in Urban America.* Bloomington, Ind.: Indiana
    University Press.

Bott, Elizabeth. 1955. "Urban Families: Conjugal roles and
    social networks." *Human Relations* 8: 345-384.

Breton, Raymond. 1964. "Institutional Completeness of Ethnic
    Communities and the Personal Relations of
    Immigrants." *American Journal of Sociology* 70: 193-
    205.

Bridge, Gary. 1995. "Gentrification, Class, and Community: A
    Social Network Approach," in *The Urban Context:
    Ethnicity, Social Networks and Situational Analysis,*
    edited by Alisdair Rogers and Steven Vertovec. Oxford,
    England: Berg Publishers.

Brint, Steven, 2001. "*Gemeinschaft* Revisited: A Critique and
    Reconstruction   of   the   Community   Concept."
    Sociological Theory 19: 1-23.

Brooks-Gunn, Jeanne, Greg J. Duncan and J. Lawrence Aber, eds. 1997. *Neighborhood Poverty*, Volume II. New York: Russell Sage Foundation.

Brubaker, Rogers. 2001. "The return of assimilation? Changing perspectives on immigration and its sequels in France, Germany, and the United States." *Ethnic and Racial Studies* 24: 531-548.

Burstein, Paul. 1976. "Social Networks and Voting: Some Israeli Data." *Social Forces* 54: 833-847.

Burt, Ronald S. 1986. "A Note on Sociometric Order in the General Social Survey Network Data." *Social Networks* 8: 293-339

------. 1987. "A Note on Strangers, Friends and Happiness." *Social Networks* 9: 311-331.

------. 2001. "Structural Holes versus Network Closure as Social Capital," in *Social Capital: Theory and Research*, edited by Nan Lin, Karen S. Cook, and Ronald S. Burt. New York: Aldine de Gruyter.

Cheng, Lucie and Philip Q. Yang. 1996. "Asians: The 'Model Minority' Deconstructed," in *Ethnic Los Angeles*, edited by Roger Waldinger and Mehdi Bozorgmehr. New York: Russell Sage Foundation.

Clark, William A.V. 1992. "Residential Preferences and Residential Choices in a Multiethnic Context." *Demography* 29: 451-466.

------. 1996. "Residential Patterns: Avoidance, Assimilation, and Succession," in *Ethnic Los Angeles*, edited by Roger Waldinger and Mehdi Bozorgmehr. New York: Russell Sage Foundation.

Coleman, James S. 1988. "Social Capital in the Creation of Human Capital." *American Journal of Sociology* 94: S95-S120

Deng, Zhong and Phillip Bonacich. 1991. "Some effects of urbanism on black social networks." *Social Networks* 13: 35-50.

Elliott, James R. 1999. "Social Isolation and Labor Market Insulation: Network and Neighborhood Effects on Less-Educated Urban Workers." *The Sociological Quarterly* 40: 199-216.

Espenshade, Thomas J., and Haishan Fu, 1997. "An Analysis of English-Language Proficiency among U.S. Immigrants." *American Sociological Review* 62: 288-305.

Espiritu, Yen Le. 1992. *Asian American Panethnicity: Bridging Institutions and Identities*. Philadelphia: Temple University Press.

Espiritu, Yen and Paul Ong. 1994. "Class Constraints on Racial Solidarity among Asian Americans," in *The New Asian Immigration in Los Angeles and Global Restructuring*, edited by Paul Ong, Edna Bonacich, and Lucie Cheng. Philadelphia: Temple University Press.

Faris, Robert E.L. 1934. "Cultural Isolation and Schizophrenic Personality." *American Journal of Sociology* 40: 155-164.

Faust, Katherine, Barbara Entwistle, Ronald R. Rindfuss, Stephen J. Walsh, and Yothin Sawangdee. 1999. "Spatial arrangement of social and economic networks among villages in Nang Rong District, Thailand." *Social Networks* 21: 311-337.

Feld, Scott L. 1981. "The Focused Organization of Social Ties." *American Journal of Sociology* 86: 1015-1035.

------. 1982. "Social Structural Determinants of Similarity among Associates." *American Sociological Review* 47: 797-801.

Feld, Scott L. and William C. Carter. 1998. "When Desegregation *Reduces* Interracial Contact: A Class Size Paradox for Weak Ties." *American Journal of Sociology* 103: 1165-1186.

Fernandez, Roberto M. and David Harris. 1992. "Social Isolation and the Underclass," in *Drugs, Crime, and Social Isolation: Barriers to Urban Opportunity*, edited by Adele V. Harrell and George E. Peterson. Washington, D.C.: The Urban Press Institute.

Fernández Kelly, M. Patricia, 1995. "Social and Cultural Capital in the Urban Ghetto: Implications for the Economic Sociology of Immigration." In *The Economic Sociology of Immigration: Essays on Networks, Ethnicity, and Entrepreneurship*, edited by Alejandro Portes. New York: Russell Sage Foundation.

Fischer, Claude S. 1982. *To Dwell Among Friends: Personal Networks in Town and City*. Chicago: University of Chicago Press.

------. 1984. *The Urban Experience*. Second edition. San Diego: Harcourt Brace Jovanovich, Inc.

Fischer, Claude S., Robert Max Jackson, C. Ann Stueve, Kathleen Gerson, Lynne McCallister Jones with Mark Baldassare. 1977. *Networks and Places: Social Relations in the Urban Setting*. New York: The Free Press.

Fischer, Claude S. and Susan L. Phillips. 1982. "Who is Alone? Social Characteristics of People With Small Networks." In *Loneliness: A Sourcebook of Current Theory, Research and Therapy*, edited by Letitia Anne Peplau and Daniel Perlman. New York: John Wiley & Sons.

Freeman, Lance. 2001. "The Effects of Sprawl on Neighborhood Social Ties." *Journal of the American Planning Association* 67: 69-77.

Freudenburg, William. 1986. "The Density of Acquaintanceship:
    An Overlooked Variable in Community Research?"
    American Journal of Sociology 92: 27-63.

Fu, Vincent. 2001. "Racial Intermarriage Pairings." *Demography*
    38: 147-159.

Furstenberg, Frank F. Jr. and Mary Elizabeth Hughes. 1997.
    "The Influence of Neighborhoods on Children's
    Development: A Theoretical Perspective and a Research
    Agenda." In *Neighborhood Poverty*, Volume II, edited
    by Jeanne Brooks-Gunn, Greg J. Duncan, and J.
    Lawrence Aber. New York: Russell Sage Foundation.

Gans, Herbert J. 1962. *The Urban Villagers: Group and Class in
    the Life of Italian-Americans.* New York: The Free Press
    of Glencoe.

------. 1967. *The Levittowners: Ways of Life and Politics in a
    New Suburban Community.* New York: Pantheon Books.

------. 1999. "Toward a Reconciliation of 'Assimilation' and
    'Pluralism': The Interplay of Acculturation and Ethnic
    Retention." In *The Handbook of International
    Migration: The American Experience.* Edited by Charles
    Hirschman, Philip Kasinitz, and Josh DeWind. New
    York: Russell Sage Foundation.

Gordon, Milton M. 1964. *Assimilation in American Life: The
    Role of Race, Religion, and National Origins.* New
    York: Oxford University Press.

Grannis, Rick. 1998. "The Importance of Trivial Streets: Tertiary
    Street Networks and Geographical Patterns of
    Residential Segregation." *American Journal of
    Sociology* 103: 1530-1564.

Granovetter, Mark. 1973. "The Strength of Weak Ties."
    American Journal of Sociology 78: 360-380.

------. 1982. "The Strength of Weak Ties: A Network Theory Revisited." In *Social Structure and Network Analysis.* Edited by Peter V. Marsden and Nan Lin. Beverly Hills: Sage Publications Inc.

Green, Gary Paul, Roger B. Hammer, and Leann M. Tigges. 2000. " 'Someone to Count on': Informal Support." In *The Atlanta Paradox*, edited by David L. Sjoquist. New York: Russell Sage Foundation.

Greenbaum, Susan D. and Paul E. Greenbaum. 1985. "The Ecology of Social Networks in Four Urban Neighborhoods." *Social Networks* 7: 47-76.

Greer, Scott. 1962. *The Emerging City*. New York: The Free Press.

Guest, Avery M., 2000. "The Mediate Community: The Nature of Local and Extra-Local Ties Within the Metropolis." *Urban Affairs Review* 35: 603-627.

Guest, Avery M., and R.S. Oropesa. 1986. "Informal Social Ties and Political Activity in the Metropolis." *Urban Affairs Quarterly* 21: 550-574.

Guest, Avery M., and Susan K. Wierzbicki. 1999. "Social Ties at the Neighborhood Level: Two Decades of GSS Evidence." *Urban Affairs Review* 35: 92-111.

Hagan, Jacqueline Maria. 1998. "Social Networks, Gender, and Immigrant Incorporation: Resources and Constraints." *American Sociological Review* 63: 55-67.

Hallinan, Maureen T. and Richard A. Williams. 1989. "Interracial Friendship Choices in Secondary Schools." *American Sociological Review* 54: 67-78.

Hamilton, Nora, and Norma Stoltz Chinchilla, 2001. *Seeking Community in a Global City: Guatemalans and Salvadorans in Los Angeles*. Philadelphia: Temple University Press.

Handlin, Oscar. 1952. *The Uprooted: The Epic Story of the Great Migrations the Made the American People.* Boston: Little, Brown and Company.

Hirschman, Charles and Luis M. Falcon. 1985. "The Educational Attainment of Religio-Ethnic Groups in the United States." *Research in Sociology of Education and Socialization* 5: 83-120.

Homans, George. 1950. *The Human Group.* New York: Harcourt, Brace & World.

Huang, Gang and Tausig, Mark. 1990. "Network Range in Personal Networks." *Social Networks* 12: 261-268.

Huckfeldt, R. Robert. 1983. "Social Contexts, Social Networks, and Urban Neighborhoods: Environmental Constraints on Friendship Choice." *American Journal of Sociology* 89: 651-669.

Hunter, Albert. 1978. "Persistence of Local Sentiments in Mass Society." *In Handbook of Contemporary Life,* edited by David Street and Associates. San Francisco: Jossey-Bass Inc.

Hurlbert, Jeanne S. 1991. "Social Networks, Social Circles, and Job Satisfaction." *Work and Occupations* 18: 415-430.

Hurlbert, Jeanne S., and Alan C. Acock, 1990. "The Effects of Marital Status on the Form and Composition of Social Networks." *Social Science Quarterly* 71: 163-174.

Hüttner, Harry J.M., Marie-josé A.M.J. Franssen, and Jean M.G. Persoon, 1990. "Homogeneity and Heterogeneity of the Effective Network in Relation to Preventive Health Behavior." In *Social Network Research: Substantive Issues and Methodological Questions,* edited by C.P.M. Knipscheer and T.C. Antonucci. Amsterdam: Swets & Zeitlinger B.V.

Hwang, Sean-Shong, and Steve H. Murdock, 1998. "Racial
  Attraction or Racial Avoidance in American Suburbs?"
  Social Forces 77: 541-566.

Johnson, James H. Jr., Elisa Jayne Bienenstock, Walter C.
  Farrell Jr., and Jennifer L. Glanville, 2000. "Bridging
  Social networks and Female Labor Force Participation in
  a Multiethnic Metropolis." In *Prismatic Metropolis:
  Inequality in Los Angeles*, edited by Lawrence D. Bobo,
  Melvin L. Oliver, James H. Johnson Jr., and Abel
  Valenzuela Jr. New York: Russell Sage Foundation.

Kalmijn, Matthijs, 1998. "Intermarriage and Homogamy:
  Causes, Patterns, Trends." *Annual Review of Sociology*
  24: 395-421.

-----, 2003. "Shared friendship networks and the life course: an
  analysis of survey data on married and cohabiting
  couples." *Social Networks* 25: 231-249

Kasarda, John D., and Morris Janowitz, 1974. "Community
  Attachment in Mass Society." *American Sociological
  Review* 39: 328-339.

Kasinitz, Philip, and Jan Rosenberg, 1996. "Missing the
  Connection: Social Isolation and Employment on the
  Brooklyn Waterfront." *Social Problems* 43: 180-196.

Kazal, Russell A., 1995. "Revisiting Assimilation: The Rise,
  Fall, and Reappraisal of a Concept in American Ethnic
  History." *American Historical Review* 100: 437-472.

Keller, Suzanne, 1968. *The Urban Neighborhood: A
  Sociological Perspective*. New York: Random House
  Inc.

Klinenberg, Eric, 2002. *Heat Wave: A Social Autopsy of Disaster
  in Chicago*. Chicago: University of Chicago Press.

Knoke, David, 1990. "Networks of Political Action: Toward
  Theory Construction." *Social Forces* 68: 1041-1063.

Korbin, Jill E., and Claudia J. Coulton, 1997. "Understanding the Neighborhood Context for Children and Families: Combining Epidemiological and Ethnographic Approaches." In *Neighborhood Poverty*, Volume II. Edited by Jeanne Brooks-Gunn, Greg J. Duncan, and J. Lawrence Aber.

Laumann, Edward O., 1973. *Bonds of Pluralism: the Form and Substance of Urban Social Networks*. New York: John Wiley & Sons.

Lee, Barrett A., and Karen E. Campbell, 1997. "Common Ground? Urban Neighborhoods as Survey Respondents See Them." *Social Science Quarterly* 78: 922-936.

------, 1999. "Neighbor Networks of Black and White Americans." In *Networks in the Global Village*. Edited by Barry Wellman. Boulder, Colo.: Westview Press.

Levitt, Peggy, 2001. The Transnational Villagers. Berkeley: University of California Press.

Liao, Tim Futing, and Gillian Stevens, 1994. "Spouses, Homogamy, and Social Networks." *Social Forces* 73: 693-707.

Lieberson, Stanley, 1980. *A Piece of the Pie: Blacks and White Immigrants Since 1880*. Berkeley: University of California Press.

Liebow, Elliot, 1967. *Tally's Corner: A Study of Negro Streetcorner Men*. Boston: Little, Brown, and Company.

Light, Ivan, and Edna Bonacich, 1988. *Immigrant Entrepreneurs: Koreans in Los Angeles, 1965-1982*. Berkeley: University of California Press.

Light, Ivan, Georges Sabagh, Mehdi Bozorgmehr, and Claudia Der-Martirosian, 1994. "Beyond the Ethnic Enclave Economy." *Social Problems* 41: 65-80.

Lin, Nan, 1986. "Conceptualizing Social Support," in *Social Support, Live Events, and Depression*, edited by Nan Lin, Alfred Dean, and Walter Ensel. Orlando, Fla.: Academic Press, Inc.

Lin, Nan, and Walter M. Ensel, 1989. "Life Stress and Health: Stressors and Resources." *American Sociological Review* 54: 382-399.

Litwak, Eugene, and Ivan Szelenyi, 1969. "Primary Group Structures and Their Functions: Kin, Neighbors, and Friends." *American Sociological Review* 34: 465-481.

Logan, John R., Richard D. Alba, and Wenquan Zhang, 2002. "Immigrant Enclaves and Ethnic Communities in New York and Los Angeles." *American Sociological Review* 67: 299-322.

Logan, John R., and Glenna D. Spitze, 1994. "Family Neighbors." *American Journal of Sociology* 100: 453-476.

Lomnitz, Larissa Adler, 1977. *Networks and Marginality: Life in a Mexican Shantytown*. New York: Academic Press.

Lopez, David E., Eric Popkin, and Edward Telles, 1996. "Central Americans: At the Bottom, Struggling to Get Ahead," in *Ethnic Los Angeles*, edited by Roger Waldinger and Mehdi Bozorgmehr. New York: Russell Sage Foundation.

Louch, Hugh, 2000. "Personal network integration: transitivity and homophily in strong-tie relations." *Social Networks* 22: 45-64.

Mahler, Sarah, 1995. *American Dreaming: Immigrant Life on the Margins*. Princeton University Press: Princeton, N.J.

Marsden, Peter V., 1987. "Core Discussion Networks of Americans." *American Sociological Review* 52: 122-131.

------, 1988. "Homogeneity in Confiding Relations." *Social Networks* 10: 57-78.

------, 1993. "The Reliability of Network Density and Composition Measures." *Social Networks* 15: 399-421.

------, 2003. "Interviewer Effects in Measuring Network Size Using a Single-Name Generator." *Social Networks* 25: 1-16.

Marsden, Peter V., and Jeanne S. Hurlbert, 1987. "Small Networks and Selectivity Bias: In the Analysis of Survey Network Data." *Social Networks* 9: 333-349.

Marsden, Peter V., and Karen E. Campbell, 1984. "Measuring Tie Strength." *Social Forces* 63: 482-501.

Massey, Douglas S., 1985. "Ethnic Residential Segregation: A Theoretical Synthesis and Empirical Review." *Sociology and Social Research* 69: 315-350.

Massey, Douglas S., Rafael Alarcón, Jorge Durand, Humberto González, 1987. *Return to Aztlan: The Social Process of International Migration from Western Mexico*. Berkeley: University of California Press.

Massey, Douglas S., Joaquin Arango, Graeme Hugo, Ali Kouaouci, Adela Pellegrino, J. Edward Taylor, 1998. *Worlds in Motion: Understanding International Migration at the End of the Millennium*. Oxford, England: Clarendon Press.

Massey, Douglas S., and Nancy A. Denton, 1987. "Trends in the Residential Segregation of Blacks, Hispanics, and Asians: 1970-1980." *American Sociological Review* 52: 802-825.

------, 1993. *American Apartheid*. Cambridge, Mass.: Harvard University Press.

McCartney, Paul, 1966. "Eleanor Rigby," in *Revolver [UK]* (The Beatles), Capitol Records.

McPherson, Miller, Lynn Smith-Lovin, and James M. Cook, 2001. "Birds of a Feather: Homophily in Social Networks." *Annual Review of Sociology* 27: 415-444.

Menjívar, Cecelia, 2000. *Fragmented Ties: Salvadoran Immigrant Networks in America*. Berkeley, Calif.: University of California Press.

Merry, Sally Engle, 1981. *Urban Danger: Life in a Neighborhood of Strangers*. Philadelphia: Temple University Press.

Milardo, Robert M., and Graham Allan, 2000. "Social Networks and Marital Relationships," in *Families as Relationships*, edited by Robert M. Milardo and Steve Duck. Chichester, England: John Wiley & Sons Ltd.

Moore, Gwen, 1990. "Structural Determinants of Men's and Women's Personal Networks." *American Sociological Review* 55: 726-735.

Moore, Joan, and Raquel Pinderhughes, eds., 1993. *In the Barrios: Latinos and the Underclass Debate*. New York: Russell Sage Foundation.

Moore, Joan, and James Diego Vigil, 1993. "Barrios in Transition," in *In the Barrios: Latinos and the Underclass Debate*. New York: Russell Sage Foundation.

Mouw, Ted, and Barbara Entwisle, 2001. "A Country of Strangers? The effect of social class, residential proximity, and mutual activities on multi-racial social segregation in schools." Paper delivered at the annual meeting of the Population Association of America, Washington, D.C.

Neckerman, Kathryn M., Prudence Carter and Jennifer Lee, 1999. "Segmented assimilation and minority cultures of mobility." *Ethnic and Racial Studies* 22: 945-965.

Ochoa, Gilda Laura, 2000. "Mexican Americans' Attitudes toward and Interactions with Mexican Immigrants: A Qualitative Analysis of Conflict and Cooperation." *Social Science Quarterly* 81: 84-105.

Oliver, Melvin L., 1988. "The Urban Black Community Network: Toward a Social Network Perspective." *The Sociological Quarterly* 29: 623-645.

Ortiz, Vilma, 1996. "The Mexican-Origin Population: Permanent Working Class or Emerging Middle Class?" In *Ethnic Los Angeles*, edited by Roger Waldinger and Mehdi Bozorgmehr. New York: Russell Sage Foundation.

Park, Robert E., 1928. "Human Migration and the Marginal Man." *American Journal of Sociology* 33: 881-893.

------, 1969 [1916]. "The City: Suggestions for the Investigation of Human Behavior in the Urban Environment." In *Classic Essays on the Culture of Cities*, edited by Richard Sennett. New York: Meredith Corp.

Pearlin, Leonard I., Morton A. Lieberman, Elizabeth G. Menaghan and Joseph T. Mullan, 1981. "The Stress Process." *Journal of Health and Social Behavior* 22: 337-356.

Perlmann, Joel, and Roger Waldinger, 1999. "Immigrants, Past and Present: A Reconsideration." In *The Handbook of International Migration: The American Experience*, edited by Charles Hirschman, Philip Kasinitz, and Josh DeWind. New York: Russell Sage Foundation.

Pessar, Patricia R., 1999. "The Role of Gender, Households, and Social Networks in the Migration Process: A Review and Appraisal." In *The Handbook of International Migration: The American Experience*, edited by Charles Hirschman, Philip Kasinitz, and Josh DeWind. New York: Russell Sage Foundation.

Philpott, Thomas Lee, 1978. *The Slum and the Ghetto: Neighborhood Deterioration and Middle-Class Reform, Chicago, 1880-1930.* New York: Oxford University Press.

Portes, Alejandro, 1998. "Social Capital: Its Origins and Applications in Modern Sociology." *Annual Review of Sociology* 24: 1-24.

-----, 2000. "The Two Meanings of Social Capital." *Sociological Forum* 15: 1-12.

Portes, Alejandro, and Robert L. Bach, 1985. *Latin Journey: Cuban and Mexican Immigrants in the United States.* Berkeley: University of California Press.

Portes, Alejandro, Luis E. Guarnizo and Patricia Landolt, 1999. "Introduction: Pitfalls and promise of an emergent research field." *Ethnic and Racial Studies* 22: 217-237.

Portes, Alejandro, and Rubén G. Rumbaut, 1996. *Immigrant America: A Portrait.* Second Edition. Berkeley: University of California Press.

------, 2001. *Legacies: The Story of the Immigrant Second Generation.* Berkeley, Calif.: University of California Press.

Portes, Alejandro, and Julia Sensenbrenner, 1998. "Embeddedness and Immigration: Notes on the Social Determinants of Economic Action." In *The New Institutionalism in Sociology.* Edited by Mary C. Brinton and Victor Nee. New York: Russell Sage Foundation.

Powell, Walter W., and Laurel Smith-Doerr, 1994. "Networks and Economic Life," in *The Handbook of Economic Sociology*, edited by Neil J. Smelser and Richard Swedberg. Princeton, N.J.: Princeton University Press.

Rainwater, Lee, 1970. *Behind Ghetto Walls: Black Families in a Federal Slum.* Chicago: Aldine Publishing Co.

Roschelle, Anne R., 1997. *No More Kin: Exploring Race, Class and Gender in Family Networks*. Thousand Oaks, Calif.: Sage Publications Inc.

Rosenfeld, Michael J., 2001. "The Salience of Pan-National Hispanic and Asian Identities in U.S. Marriage Markets." *Demography* 38: 161-175

Ross, Catherine E., John Mirowsky, and Shana Pribesh, 2001. "Powerlessness and the Amplification of Threat: Neighborhood Disadvantage, Disorder, and Mistrust." *American Sociological Review* 66: 568-591.

Rossi, Peter, 1980. *Why Families Move*. Second edition. Beverly Hills, Calif.: Sage Publications.

Ruan, Danching, 1998. "The content of the General Social Survey discussion networks: an exploration of General Social Survey discussion name generator in a Chinese context." *Social Networks* 20: 247-264.

Rumbaut, Rubén G., 1999. "Assimilation and Its Discontents: Ironies and Paradoxes." In *The Handbook of International Migration: The American Experience*. Edited by Charles Hirschman, Philip Kasinitz, and Josh DeWind. New York: Russell Sage Foundation.

Rytina, Steve, and David L. Morgan, 1982. "The Arithmetic of Social Relations: The Interplay of Category and Network." *American Journal of Sociology* 88: 88-113.

Sampson, Robert J., 1988. "Local Friendship Ties and Community Attachment in Mass Society: A Multilevel Systemic Model." *American Sociological Review* 53: 766-779.

Sampson, Robert J., Jeffrey D. Morenoff, and Felton Earls, 1999. "Beyond Social Capital: Spatial Dynamics of Collective Efficacy for Children." *American Sociological Review* 64: 633-660.

Sandefur, Rebecca L., and Edward O. Laumann, 1998. "A Paradigm for Social Capital." *Rationality and Society* 10: 481-501.

Sanders, Jimy, Victor Nee, and Scott Sernau, 2002. "Asian Immigrants' Reliance on Social Ties in a Multiethnic Labor Market." *Social Forces* 81: 281-314.

Sassen, Saskia, 1990. "Economic Restructuring and the American City." *Annual Review of Sociology* 16: 465-490.

Scherzer, Kenneth A., 1992. *The Unbounded Community: Neighborhood Life and Social Structure in New York City, 1830-1875*. Durham, N.C.: Duke University Press.

Schiller, Nina Glick, 1999. "Transmigrants and Nation-States: Something Old and Something New in the U.S. Immigrant Experience." In *The Handbook of International Migration: The American Experience.* Edited by Charles Hirschman, Philip Kasinitz, and Josh DeWind. New York: Russell Sage Foundation.

Shaw, Clifford R., and Henry McKay, 1942. *Juvenile Delinquency and Urban Areas*. Chicago: University of Chicago Press.

Shrum, Wesley, Neil H. Cheek, Jr., and Saundra MacD. Hunter, 1988. "Friendship in School: Gender and Racial Homophily." *Sociology of Education* 61: 227-239.

Sigelman, Lee, Timothy Bledsoe, Susan Welch, and Michael W. Combs, 1996. "Making Contact? Black-White Social Interaction in an Urban Setting." *American Journal of Sociology* 101: 1306-1332.

Simmel, Georg, [1922] 1955. *Conflict & The Web of Group-Affiliations*. New York: The Free Press.

------, 1950. *The Sociology of Georg Simmel*. Translated and edited by Kurt H. Wolff. New York: The Free Press.

Smith, James P. and Barry Edmonston, editors, 1997. *The New Americans: Economic, Demographic, and Fiscal Effects of Immigration*. Washington, D.C.: National Academy Press.

Smith, Michael, 2001. *Transnational Urbanism: Locating Globalization*. London: Blackwell Publishers.

Stack, Carol B., 1974. *All Our Kin: Strategies for Survival in a Black Community*. New York: Harper & Row.

StataCorp., 2001. *Stata User's Guide. Release 7*. Stata Press: College Station, Texas.

Stevens, Gillian, 1992. "The Social and Demographic Context of Language Use in the United States." *American Sociological Review* 57: 171-185.

Straits, Bruce C., 1991. "Bringing Strong Ties Back in Interpersonal Gateways to Political Information and Influence." *Public Opinion Quarterly* 55: 432-448.

------, 1996. "Ego-net diversity: Same- and cross-sex coworker ties." *Social Networks* 18: 29-45.

------, 2000. "Ego's important discussants or significant people: an experiment in varying the wording of personal network name generators." *Social Networks* 22: 123-140.

Suttles, Gerald D., 1968. *The Social Order of the Slum: Ethnicity and Territory in the Inner City*. Chicago: University of Chicago Press.

Thoits, Peggy A., 1984. "Explaining Distributions of Psychological Vulnerability: Lack of Social Support in the Face of Life Stress." *Social Forces* 63: 453-481.

Thomas, William I., and Florian Znaniecki, 1984. *The Polish Peasant in Europe and America*, edited and abridged by Eli Zaretsky. Urbana, Ill.: University of Illinois Press.

Tienda, Marta, 1991. "Poor People and Poor Places: Deciphering Neighborhood Effects on Poverty Outcomes." In *Macro-micro Links in Sociology*, edited by Joan Huber. Newbury Park, Calif.: Sage Publications.

Tilly, Charles, 1990. "Transplanted Networks," in *Immigration Reconsidered*, edited by Virginia Yans-McLaughlin. New York: Oxford University Press.

Tönnies, Ferdinand, 1963 [1887]. *Community and Society*. Translated and edited by Charles Loomis. New York: Harper & Row.

Tseng, Yen-Fen, 1995. "Beyond 'Little Taipei': The Development of Taiwanese Immigrant Businesses in Los Angeles." *International Migration Review* 19: 33-58.

United States Department of Commerce, Bureau of the Census, 1993. *1990 Census of Population. Social and Economic Characteristics, Metropolitan Areas*. Washington: U.S. Government Printing Office.

Verbrugge, Lois M., 1977. "The Structure of Adult Friendship Choices." *Social Forces* 56:576-597.

Waldinger, Roger, 1993. "The Ethnic Enclave Debate Revisited." *International Journal of Urban and Regional Research* 17: 444-452.

------, 1999. "Network, Bureaucracy, and Exclusion: Recruitment and Selection in an Immigrant Metropolis." In *Immigration and Opportunity: Race, Ethnicity and Employment in the United States*, edited by Frank D. Bean and Stephanie Bell-Rose. New York: Russell Sage Foundation.

Waldinger, Roger, and Mehdi Bozorgmehr, editors, 1996. *Ethnic Los Angeles*. New York: Russell Sage Foundation.

Wasserman, Stanley, and Katherine Faust, 1994. *Social Network Analysis: Methods and Applications*. Cambridge, UK: Cambridge University Press.

Wellman, Barry, 1979. "The Community Question: The Intimate Networks of East Yorkers." *American Journal of Sociology* 84: 1201-1231.

------, 1996. "Are Personal Communities Local? A Dumptarian Reconsideration." *Social Networks* 18: 347-354.

------, editor, 1999. *Networks in the Global Village: Life in Contemporary Communities*. Boulder, Colo.: Westview Press.

Wellman, Barry, and S.D. Berkowitz, 1988. "Introduction: Studying Social Structures." In *Social Structures: A Network Approach*, edited by Barry Wellman and S.D. Berkowitz. Cambridge, England: Cambridge University Press.

Wellman, Barry, and Barry Leighton, 1979. "Networks, Neighborhoods, and Communities: Approaches to the Study of the Community Question." *Urban Affairs Quarterly* 14: 363-390.

Wellman, Barry, and Scot Wortley, 1990. "Different Strokes from Different Folks: Community Ties and Social Support." *American Journal of Sociology* 96: 558-588.

White, Harrison C., Scott A. Boorman, and Ronald L. Brieger, 1976. "Social Structure from Multiple Networks: I. Blockmodels of Roles and Positions." *American Journal of Sociology* 81: 730-780.

White, Michael J., and Sharon Sassler, 2000. "Judging Not Only by Color: Ethnicity, Nativity, and Neighborhood Attainment." *Social Science Quarterly* 81: 997-1013.

Wilson, Kenneth L., and Alejandro Portes, 1980. "Immigrant Enclaves: An Analysis of the Labor Market Experiences of Cubans in Miami." *American Journal of Sociology* 86: 295-319.

Wilson, William Julius, 1978. *The Declining Significance of Race: Blacks and Changing American Institutions.* Chicago: University of Chicago Press.

------, 1987. *The Truly Disadvantaged: The Inner City, the Underclass, and Public Policy.* Chicago: University of Chicago Press.

Wireman, Peggy, 1984. *Urban Neighborhoods, Networks and Families: New Forms for Old Values.* Lexington, Mass.: Lexington Books.

Wirth, Louis, 1956 [1928]. *The Ghetto.* Chicago: University of Chicago Press.

------, 1938. "Urbanism as a Way of Life." *American Journal of Sociology* 44: 3-24.

Yancey, William L., Eugene P. Ericksen and Richard N. Juliani, 1976. "Emergent Ethnicity: A Review and Reformulation." *American Sociological Review* 41: 391-403.

Yinger, John, 1995. *Closed Doors, Opportunities Lost: The Continuing Costs of Housing Discrimination.* New York: Russell Sage Foundation.

Zang, Xiaowei, and Riaz Hassan, 1996. "Residential Choices of Immigrants in Australia." *International Migration* 34: 567-582.

Zelinsky, Wilbur, and Barrett A. Lee, 1998. "Heterolocalism: An Alternative Model of the Sociospatial Behaviour of Immigrant Ethnic Communities." *International Journal of Population Geography* 4: 281-298.

Zhou, Min, 1992. *Chinatown: The Socioeconomic Potential of an Urban Enclave*. Philadelphia: Temple University Press.

------, 1999. "Segmented Assimilation: Issues, Controversies, and Recent Research." In *The Handbook of International Migration: The American Experience*. Edited by Charles Hirschman, Philip Kasinitz, and Josh DeWind. New York: Russell Sage Foundation.

Zhou, Min, and Carl L. Bankston III, 1998. *Growing Up American: How Vietnamese Children Adapt to Life in the United States*. New York: Russell Sage Foundation.

Zhou, Yu, 1998. "How Do Places Matter? A Comparative Study of Chinese Ethnic Economies in Los Angeles and New York City." *Urban Geography* 19: 531-553.

Index

strong ties, 9-11, 13-18,
22, 34, 41, 60-65, 69,
112-116, 120
weak ties, 13, 22-23, 116
with neighbors, 17, 34-35,
44, 77-90
with kin, 16, 67-76, 113
Spatial assimilation, 6-7, 94-
95, 100-104, 108-110,
115
Spitze, Glenna D., 78
Stata, 125
Stevens, Gillian, 2, 6-7, 9, 11,
129
Structural assimilation, 6-9,
108, 110, 115
Stack, Carol B., 14, 39, 68
Straits, Bruce C., 52-53, 129-
130
Suttles, Gerald D., 36-37
Szelenyi, Ivan, 11, 14, 68

T

Tausig, Mark, 129
Telles, Edward, 49
Thoits, Peggy A., 26
Thomas, W. I., 1, 36
Tienda, Marta, 33
Tigges, Leann M., 130
Tilly, Charles, 2, 6, 37
Tönnies, Ferdinand, 30
Tseng, Yen-Fen, 6, 95
Turner, Eugene, 49, 110

V

Verbrugge, Lois M., 15
Vigil, James Diego, 42

W

Waldinger, Roger, 2-4, 7, 9,
19, 45-47
Wasserman, Stanley, 23
Wellman, Barry, 7, 11, 14, 17,
21-23, 30, 32- 36, 55,
79, 81-82, 104, 116-
117
White, Harrison C., 22
White, Michael J., 134
Wierzbicki, Susan K., 6-7, 9
Williams, Richard A., 15
Wilson, Kenneth L, 31
Wilson, William Julius, 4, 16,
27-28, 32, 40-42, 115,
120
Wireman, Peggy, 54, 131
Wirth, Louis, 1, 3, 30, 36, 42
Wortley, Scot, 7, 11, 14, 104

Y

Yancey, William L., 13, 15
Yang, Philip Q., 47, 49
Yinger, John, 95

Z

Zang, Xiaowei, 32
Zelinsky, Wilbur, 6-7, 30, 36,
94-95, 109-110
Zhang, Wenquan, 6, 95
Zhou, Min, 4, 7, 9, 12, 23, 27,
29, 31, 33-34, 37, 45,
66, 120
Zhou, Yu, 3
Znaniecki, Florian, 1, 36